# HOUSE WITHOUT WALLS

## MARGARET BLAIR YOUNG

Deseret Book Company
Salt Lake City, Utah

**Library of Congress Cataloging-in-Publication Data**

Young, Margaret Blair, 1955–
    House without walls / by Margaret Blair Young.
      p.  cm.
    ISBN 0-87579-394-0
    I. Title.
PS3575.0825L3   1991
813'.54—dc20
                                       91-8322
                                         CIP

Printed in the United States of America

10   9   8   7   6   5   4   3   2   1

*To*
*Kaila Corinne, Robert Daren,*
*and Julia Ruth:*
*children of promise*

# HOUSE WITHOUT WALLS

# ACKNOWLEDGMENTS

My thanks to Ben Urrutia for his assistance and to Bruce Jorgensen—one of the best writers and editors I know—for his generous help in my early revisions and for his constant encouragement. Finally, thanks to Bruce Wilson Young, who is not only my spell-checker, editor, teacher, and critic, but my best friend and husband.

I also wish to acknowledge my Jewish friends and former students, who freely shared their culture and traditions with me. Though my own Latter-day Saint convictions will be apparent in this novel, I hope my love for Jewish history and the Jewish way of life will be equally clear.

# INTRODUCTION

## BRUCE YOUNG

In 1986 I spent a week in Berlin for a conference on Shakespeare. I remember one face especially from that week, the face of an East German border guard at the Berlin Wall. He was a young man with rosy cheeks and round wire-rim glasses. He wore a cap and a heavy black coat and carried some kind of gun, what looked to me like a machine gun. Earlier in the week I had gone into East Berlin with a bus full of fellow academics from various countries. But this time I entered East Berlin on my own. After having my passport examined at Checkpoint Charlie, I walked into what was officially "the Soviet sector." A few hours later, on my way back to Checkpoint Charlie, I became confused and wasn't sure where to enter the checkpoint building to return to West Berlin. That is when I saw the guard. I looked at him, hoping he would direct me. He motioned with his gun toward the entrance, but

I still couldn't see where exactly to go. He kept motioning and yelled, "Hier! Hier!" I finally found the entryway, but my heart was pounding. Not that I had been seriously afraid of being shot. I'm sure many tourists have made similar mistakes. But I remembered the fear in the young guard's eyes. I knew he would be in trouble if I did something seriously wrong. He might even have to shoot or else face punishment himself.

When I think of that young man now, I realize he must no longer be working as a border guard. The Berlin Wall no longer officially exists; much of it has been taken down. I hope the young man was able to take part in the festivities that marked the end of the wall. I would like to imagine him now much happier, more relaxed than he was when I met him.


When my wife wrote this novel—the first draft was completed about seven years ago—the Berlin Wall still stood. Its fall and the other amazing events of the last few years were as yet hardly imaginable. We were told that someday barriers would fall, and we were asked to pray for that day. But almost no one thought the hoped-for day would come so soon, so suddenly.

Much of this novel is set in Germany, and it deals with some of the terrible events that have taken place there in this century. Perhaps even in the 1980s the wounds inflicted by these events were too fresh, too painful. Some who looked at the novel felt the time was not right to publish it. Perhaps the book would be misunderstood, and such misunderstanding might impede the progress being made, slowly and tentatively, to breach the walls separating Latter-day Saints from other people.

But our world has changed dramatically since this book was first drafted. Suddenly, as if overnight, we have many more opportunities for making connections, greater freedom to share our views without fear of being misunderstood. The time seems right to look again at the issues confronted in this book. Now that the Berlin Wall has fallen, now that political barriers have fallen or are beginning to fall, we are perhaps ready to tear down other walls that separate us, the kinds of walls you will find spoken of in this novel.

These walls include not only the literal, physical walls — such as the Berlin Wall — that separate people but also the spiritual and emotional walls, the walls of prejudice, misunderstanding, hatred, and sin. There is also the wall — or perhaps the veil — that separates the living and the dead, a wall that can become very thin in the temple and at those moments when we remember those who have gone before or when we become aware of the concern felt for us by loved ones on the other side.

My aim here is to remind you who read this novel of the connections between the fictional world my wife has created and the world in which we are living. The pain and joy recreated in this book have happened — are happening even now — to real people. The evils committed in our century have resulted in suffering and bitterness and hardness of heart, much of it still unfinished and unresolved. These consequences are felt not only by those who suffered the wrongs but by those who committed them or overlooked or tried to overlook them. The consequences are felt, too, by the families and friends of the victims and the wrongdoers. All of us, in fact, participate knowingly or unknowingly in the effects of the awful events of our century. These events have built walls — political divisions, bitterness and fear, hatred and suspicion, the pain of guilt or the hardness of self-justification and willful ignorance. When seen in human terms, the problems of our world call out for the age-old, eternal means by which human pain has always been remedied: repentance and forgiveness.

During my week in Berlin, I was reminded vividly of the terrible events of the 1930s and 1940s. In East Berlin I saw a synagogue whose windows had been broken during the rampage of anti-Semitic violence known as *Kristallnacht*; the synagogue had been further damaged by bombing during the war. I saw the place where Nazis had burned thousands of books. In West Berlin I walked to the Plötzensee Prison, where enemies of the Nazi regime had been held and executed. I looked into the execution room and saw the very place where a young Mormon, Helmuth Huebner, was beheaded for telling his fellow Germans things they did not want to know about their government. I remember Helmuth's face, too, from the pamphlet now available at the site. He was a young man, only seventeen, with a fearless, idealistic look in his eyes. My wife has described him elsewhere as "a young kid who had cocked his head during Sunday School, had flirted with girls, maybe thought about getting married, certainly thought about doing something important with his life. . . . A quarterbackish kid with dark, wavy hair, light eyes, and dreams. Youth itself at the brink of possibility, full of innocence and purpose."

The events of the thirties and forties were especially painful — are still painful in remembrance — for Jews. During the conference in Berlin, I made friends with a Jew from Canada. Visiting Germany was hard for him. It was difficult for him to think of that country without thinking of the suffering and death of millions of his people. But he had decided to go. During his days in Berlin he visited the same sites I did and doubtless felt the pain and horror associated with some of those sites much more deeply than I was able to. But he also made German friends, felt the goodness of the German people, and saw evidence of Germany's contributions to the world. He must have been reminded, as I was, that many Germans—Jews and non-Jews—had suffered at the hands of fellow Germans, both during and after the war, and that German lives had also been disrupted and destroyed by Allied bombing during the war and by Soviet tanks afterwards. For my Jewish friend, the visit to Berlin was both a reminder of appalling events and also a way of achieving a measure of reconciliation. For him, some walls were torn down, even in this city divided by the famous wall.

For Latter-day Saints, as for other human beings, it is tempting to divide the world into "us" and "them," "good guys" and "bad guys," friends and enemies. But our calling to share the gospel with all nations helps us transcend our narrow insularity as it reminds us that our fellow humans are our sisters and brothers. We know that, belonging to the kingdom of God, our fellow citizens include people of many nations. The revelations about our eternal nature help us see that our connections with our brothers and sisters are much deeper than our differences.

Temple work also links us with brothers and sisters of other nations and races. We receive ordinances as if we actually were another person. We give a voice to those who are now without earthly voices. We speak in their behalf. Too often this activity—redemptive for us as well as for the dead we represent—becomes routine. But at times, as the Spirit enhances our sensitivities, we are aware of the literal reality of the persons whose names we are bearing.

The names of some of those killed in the Holocaust, the Nazi destruction of the Jews, have been placed in files at the Provo Temple. On several occasions my wife and I have asked

for names from those files. We look at the date of birth on the
slip given us and estimate how old the person must have been
when taken to one of the death camps. As we make covenants
for these victims of the Holocaust, we imagine the suffering,
the despair, they felt. We want intensely to help somehow in
the process of their redemption. These people were herded
together and killed en masse. There was something terribly
anonymous in their persecution and murder. They were treated
not as individuals but as nameless members of a despised race.
Temple work, we have felt, somehow reverses that process.
Those who were destroyed en masse are redeemed one by
one. Those deprived of names and voices are given names and
voices again. We think of them as individuals, one at a time.
We contemplate their names, try to imagine their faces: Samuel
Misch, born in 1890, fifty years old in 1940, a middle-aged Jew
with a German surname; Henni Van der Meer, born in 1896,
her Dutch name indicating that she, like Anne Frank, was taken
from Holland to a death camp. As we do temple work for this
man and this woman, we are reminded that God is a God of
both the living and the dead, that all souls are precious to him.
The hope of a glorious resurrection, made possible by our
Savior's offer of himself, becomes very real as we think of these
persons who were deprived of a voice, deprived of life, for a
time deprived of hope.

My wife and I, like many others, have felt great joy as we
have seen the Berlin Wall crumble, families reunite, freedom
expand, conflict — at least in some parts of the world — diminish.
The miraculous events of the end of the 1980s and the beginning of the 1990s bear witness that God is mindful of his
children. The Atonement, that great covenant between heaven
and earth, is for all times, all places; for every nation, kindred,

tongue, and people. The events in Eastern Europe—the fall of totalitarian regimes, the reform and liberalization in the Soviet Union, the building of a temple in what was then East Germany, the opening of missionary work there and in Poland, Czechoslovakia, Hungary, even the Soviet Union—these events, we feel, are no accidents, nor are they the result of merely human efforts. For years, thousands have been praying in these countries and elsewhere, and despite political and religious oppression, many have worshipped in secret, have longed for scriptures, have quoted passages from the Bible to each other from memory. In response to the prayers and faith of these people and of believers around the world, hearts have been softened and doors have been opened.

Especially during the last two years, we have seen miracles. The people of countries in Eastern Europe have patiently and courageously called for changes. Free elections are being held in several of those countries. New freedoms—political, economic, artistic, and religious—are being extended. New responsibilities and possibilities are being offered. And new leaders are rising as these countries embark on new paths. Addressing his people on January 1, 1990, Vaclav Havel, newly elected president of Czechoslovakia, said, "Everywhere in the world, people were surprised how these malleable, humiliated, cynical citizens of Czechoslovakia, who seemingly believed in nothing, found the tremendous strength within a few weeks to cast off the totalitarian system, in an entirely peaceful and dignified manner. We ourselves are surprised at it. Where did young people who had never known another system get their longing for truth, their love of freedom? How is it possible that so many people immediately understood what to do and that none of them needed any advice or instructions?"

The crowd who listened to him in Wenceslas Square later

broke into song. "May peace be with this land," they sang. "Let hate, envy, fear, and conflict pass. May they pass, may they pass, may they pass!"

After the burial of Jesus, Mary Magdalene and the other Mary came to see the sepulchre: "And, behold, there was a great earthquake: for the angel of the Lord descended from heaven, and came and rolled back the stone from the door, and sat upon it. His countenance was like lightning, and his raiment white as snow. . . . And the angel . . . said unto the women, Fear not ye: for I know that ye seek Jesus, which was crucified. He is not here: for he is risen, as he said." (Matthew 28:2–6). The rolling back of that stone removed the wall that had stood between the living and the dead, between sinners and their hope for salvation. In the past few years, we have seen events that are startlingly similar to the rolling back of that stone. The Berlin Wall was another barrier between people — between families, between ideologies, between freedom and bondage. Even as this concrete barrier has come down and great reunions have been allowed between brothers and sisters on both sides, so was the wall between life and death undone in the resurrection of Jesus. We who have laid or who will lay loved ones in the grave have an assurance that the wall separating us will not be permanent. There are sweet reunions to come.

The scriptures use the image of walls to describe the separation of Jew from Gentile, and of all of us from our Heavenly Father. Through the gospel and through the atonement of Christ, these walls are broken down. Indeed, the word *atonement* means literally "At-One-Ment." Christ's atonement has the potential to bring us to a state of oneness with each other and with God. Paul wrote in Ephesians, chapter 2: "But now in Christ Jesus ye who sometimes were far off are made nigh by the blood of Christ. For he is our peace, who hath made both one, and hath broken down the middle wall of partition between us. . . . Now therefore ye are no more strangers and foreigners, but fellowcitizens with the saints, and of the household of God" (vv. 13–14, 19).

That "middle wall of partition" is still in process of coming down. There is still much prejudice and misunderstanding. Conflict, pride, and hatred still rule in too many places and in too many hearts. Many in our world are still struggling for their liberties. Even the nations of Eastern Europe are not yet fully free but are at the beginning of their freedoms, as are we all in our individual lives. There are trials to come. How well we pass through those trials will depend on the strength of our faith, the vibrancy of our hope, the depth of our charity for all of God's children.

The characters in this novel are fictional. They have been imagined — vividly imagined — from hints my wife has found in her reading and other experience. But, though they are fictional, their experiences and emotions are real. You will see them experiencing things, both wondrous and terrible things, that real people have experienced in our world, in our century. I believe you will come to love these characters; you will suffer and rejoice with them. Our hope is that the feelings you have as you read will lead you to greater tolerance and understanding for the real people you encounter, and that you, like the characters in this novel, will have the courage and love to tear down the walls that separate you from others.

# PART ONE

## SARAH AND ABRAHAM

# CHAPTER 1

## HAMBURG, SPRING 1945

Emaciated, her cropped brown hair flecked with gray, Sarah Sinasohn rounded the corner and stopped cold. Her eyes surveyed a house — her house, which rose like a charred monolith from stinking ruins. Sarah blinked, squinted, blinked again. "How did you survive?" she whispered, walking to it, touching its dirty bricks. She breathed a word from her past: "Mama."

The wind moaned.

Mama, of course, was gone, dead. Mama's voice would never again fill the kitchen as she sang over the *challah* bread for the Sabbath. Mama was gone.

And Papa was gone. They had taken him too. They had called him "Aaron the Jew," though he kept none of the Jewish laws, and they had taken him, with her brothers David and Moses, and made them all dead and gone. All gone. All but this house.

She looked for the little willow tree that once had seemed to speak to her. It was not there, but she could see clearly where it had been. A small black pit marked its grave.

That tree had saved her. She wouldn't have joined the Mormons if the tree had not "spoken" to her. But (helped by her imagination) it had spoken, had seemed to answer her prayers and tell her the Mormons were right and their gospel true. It had saved her, for she would not have survived the war had it not been for the Mormons. She had been preserved. Now she was a relic from the past, lost beside her own house. And the willow was gone.

She entered. The smell of death was more rancid inside than out. There were holes in the walls. She thought that rats and mice must have sought refuge there and died. She was sure if she looked in the holes she would see their piled bones. She stared at the empty fireplace, remembering only vaguely how comfortable its light once had been. She sat beside it, trying to conjure some sort of vision from the past. Nothing came but a memory of the two Mormon missionaries she had met only once. And even that was blurred.

It was the winter of her twelfth year. The missionaries had knocked as though knocking were a natural, innocent thing for strangers to do to a Jewish door. She had calmly answered and let them in. Yes, there had been a time — long, long ago — when one answered knocks at one's door without fear. From the fireplace she could see the very door she had answered.

An icy wind had blown inside and made her shiver as she regarded the two red-cheeked, red-nosed Americans. In accented German, the taller one, a bearlike boy, had said, "We're elders of The Church of Jesus Christ of Latter-day Saints, and we have a message for your family. Is your mother or father home?"

She had told them no, but she invited them in to warm themselves anyway, and they had sat on the wooden chairs beside the fire and told her about Jesus Christ and Joseph Smith. Then her pious brother David had entered and rigidly shook the missionaries' hands.

"We're representatives of The Church of Jesus Christ of Latter-day Saints, and we have a message for you," the other elder—a skinny, blond fellow—said. "It's the message of the restored gospel of Jesus Christ."

Slowly, David lifted his head and brought himself to his full height. "We're Jews in this house," he said. "Perhaps the kingdom of God has come for you. Perhaps you think it has. But for us—not yet."

"The scriptures say, 'He was despised and rejected of men, a man of sorrows and acquainted with grief . . .'" said the bearlike missionary.

"You quote that scripture you have taken from us. We know—I know—about being despised and rejected. If I didn't know, then perhaps I could accept your doctrine and the easy Christian life," said David, his voice brittle.

The missionaries smiled—both of them together, as though they had rehearsed it. "May we bless this house before we leave it?" the big missionary asked.

David shook his head. "You leave now, please. Pray outside, if you want. A Christian prayer does not fit in a Jewish house. Go outside, please."

The Americans left, and Sarah heard them praying on the other side of the door—that door—blessing the house, asking that it be preserved, as the widow's shelter in Jericho had been. And this before the war.

Then David studied her as a lion would a fawn. "You will never let them or anyone like them into this house," he whisper-yelled. "The Christians have massacred us more than once. Never again will you let them enter. Never again!"

She nodded, but David did not stop. He shouted and shouted and finally grabbed her forearm and squeezed it hard, saying, "You leave them alone and pray that they will leave us alone!" As though he had already foreseen it. As though he already knew.

She nodded, as she was nodding now, again and again, head bobbing up and down, rhythmically, hypnotically. In her mind the words: "Yes, David. Yes."

Yes. All that had happened. She remembered it. Remembered the missionaries blessing the house. Remembered them. Remembered David.

She sat on the dirty floor. The memories came more vividly and, for a moment, cleared the room of death.

# CHAPTER 2

## HAMBURG, 1929

The Hilde Goldstein Beth Yacov School for Girls, in which Sarah's mother enrolled her after much remonstration from both Sarah and Aaron, was a two-room box with a star of David painted on its facade. Sarah hated it instantly. The hall separating the two rooms was bare and shadowy. The classrooms (one for upper grades, one for lower) were bleak, the desks unevenly varnished and scratched. Rabbi Abraham Cohen was the principal of the school and the art teacher. Two other teachers, both men, taught the girls Hebrew, Jewish law, history, language, and mathematics. Sarah found them all humorless. She disliked the custom of standing whenever the rabbi entered the classroom. She disliked the preoccupation with things Jewish. She disliked the classes and the school, inside and out.

Rabbi Cohen, though mild-eyed and soft-spoken at first

meeting, seemed especially severe. Judging from his dark hair and smooth face, he was a young man — but he acted old. When a student behaved badly, Rabbi Cohen's mild eyes flared; his soft, rich voice built to a thunderous crescendo, he escorted the naughty one to his office (a glass-enclosed section of one of the classrooms), and then walked briskly down the hall, as though remaining with such a miscreant would taint his perfect soul. Nonetheless, moments after such a scene, Rabbi Cohen could greet an official with the most unctuous cordiality, eyes brimming again with soft emotion.

As the school year progressed, Sarah experienced the rabbi's anger more than once. Indeed, before the first week of school was over, she had a reputation for being a rebellious, incorrigible girl, and she braced herself whenever she saw the rabbi, even before class had begun. When she was escorted to his office, he generally did not even look at her but said methodically, "Well, Sarah, I wonder if we will ever be able to have a pleasant conversation, you and I."

It was school policy that the student should confess her misdeeds and apologize for them. Most of the girls did that with bowed heads and teary voices. Sarah tried to imitate the pose, but found the rabbi's eyes too magnetic. She could not bow her head.

"You drew cartoons — CARTOONS — during Hebrew class," he accused her once. That was the cue for her to bow her head and cry, but she found her eyes riveted to his. She could not force tears, either, and offered only a laconic shrug.

"I don't like Hebrew," she said.

"What does that matter? You are a Jew. Your scriptures — God's word to YOU — are written in Hebrew."

"Then maybe I don't want to be a Jew," she murmured, shrugging again and looking briefly away.

"Well, you have no choice in that, have you. You were born to Jewish parents; therefore, you are a Jew. Despite your attitude, God has chosen you."

"My parents speak German, not Hebrew."

The rabbi accused her of having no conscience or sense of respect. Sarah forced her head downwards and tried to look sorrowful, tried again to work up some tears. But a fit of giggling took her and, though she pretended to be sobbing, the rabbi saw her grin. The hairs of his black beard quivered. As a parting line before his traditional walk of disgust down the hall, he told her to stay in his office the rest of the day and to copy by hand the entire Hallel and the first chapter of Leviticus — in Hebrew, of course.

She obeyed, and when she had finished, absently drew a caricature of Rabbi Cohen rushing down the hall, hat flying from his head. She was not aware that she had forgotten to remove the caricature from her copywork and did not think of it until the rabbi invited her into his office the following day. There, on the center of his desk, was her artwork.

"Hello, Sarah," he said.

"Good morning, Rabbi Cohen."

"I see you decided to do some extra work, in addition to the Hallel and the verses from Leviticus."

Her cheeks warmed.

"Yes?" He smiled. "Don't be frightened. I have not called you in to reprimand you," he said. "Not this time. You have received more than your share of reprimands from me, yes? And I'm sure the last one will not be — will not be — the last one. It seems as though you and I are destined to know each other well, unfortunately. But I want you to understand that your art is good, even considering its subject. I would much prefer discussing your artwork to scolding you. Let us see if our next meeting can be about art, shall we?"

There was no brisk walking this time, and Sarah felt wicked and small. "May I have it back?" she said.

Again the rabbi smiled. "There are many artists in the world today, some good, some bad. But one never knows which will become famous or why. This little drawing may be quite valuable someday, and I intend to keep it." His smile broadened. Sarah noticed with an embarrassed shock that he was not bad looking.

# CHAPTER 3

Abraham Cohen was the fourth in a family line of rabbis. It was the Jewish custom that every firstborn male child should belong to God. The father paid a token sum for his son's release to his care.

Abraham was the firstborn of his father's family. Though the elder Rabbi Cohen, Samuel, had fulfilled the requirements of the Law in buying his boy back, Abraham understood throughout his life that he was expected to become a servant of God, a scholar of Judaism, a rabbi. He fulfilled the expectations magnificently. He not only learned the writings of past scholars and prophets—the *nauvey*—but loved them.

As a child, he would watch his father in the morning, enveloped in the white prayer shawl with black stripes, leather boxes strapped to his forehead and left arm, reciting morning prayers. The shawl had knots and fringes numbering 613, or the number of all God's commandments and of all the organs and veins of the body. The black stripes signified the destruction of the temple. The leather boxes, or tefillin, contained parchment scrolls and the story of the Exodus. Samuel Cohen was a man of God. He walked in the Law.

Abraham prided himself in wearing his yarmulke—the skullcap—faithfully, and often repeated to himself upon donning it, "God is always above."

His mother, who died of a cerebral hemorrhage when Abraham was twenty-two years old, was also a keeper of the Jewish way. Her light, mellifluous voice indicated that all was well as she prayed, eyes covered, on Sabbath eve and lit the candles. He remembered her whenever he smelled a Jewish kitchen. On Fridays, she served warm, braided *challah* bread, a cloth covering it as the dew from Heaven had covered the Israelites' manna. During Chanukah she served *latkes*—flat pancakes. During Pesach, her meals were exquisite and varied and more appreciated after the fast. All the food she prepared was consecrated by her love and by its meaning in the traditions the family shared.

With such parents, it was not hard for Abraham to embrace the faith and extend his hands to his ancestors who had bequeathed him their traditions. But to feel their touch, to actually hear the prophets and psalm writers prompting him with their poems, whispering their words to him—that came after years of study and meditation. And when he was ordained a rabbi in 1927, young Abraham Cohen, barely twenty-five years old, wept with joy.

A match had been made for him two weeks before he was ordained. The girl, Deborah Fried, was from a nearby village. He had seen her at shul on a few occasions and knew he would love her because she was so like his late mother. Deborah's voice, too, was light and sweet. She had pale skin, golden eyes, and thick, brown hair. She was, like his mother, a modest woman, her clothes simple, her complexion clear, unembellished.

They were married four weeks after Yom Kippur. Within a month of the wedding, Deborah was pregnant.

Their first child, a son, was born in the sixth month of Deborah's term. Abraham gave him the name Daniel and took him in his arms. The boy struggled to fill his unready lungs with air, looked Abraham directly in the eyes, and died.

Deborah conceived again six months later, and miscarried seven weeks afterwards. Almost immediately, she conceived again, and almost immediately miscarried. The strain of the fruitless pregnancies began to show on her body and face. She looked pale, exhausted, used up. She prayed day and night for a child. Now, in 1929, she was beginning to bloom again with seed.

Abraham praised the Lord for his mercies, gave glory even for the grief he and Deborah had suffered. "For how I love her now," he said to the Master of the Universe, "after the lives we have had and lost, after the blood and tears we have mixed in our two years together."

Abraham was stretching at his office desk forty minutes after school had dismissed when his friend and neighbor, old Rav Hillel, rushed into the classroom and called his name, turning to the right and to the left but keeping his legs firmly planted, slightly apart, on the floor.

Rav Hillel was an intense man who imagined great anti-Semitic plots and could conjure a conspiracy in his mind if the newspaper boy did not greet him properly. Twice in the last year he had barged in on Abraham before the start or after the dismissal of school and announced monumental prophecies, always interpreted from his own dreams. Indeed, he fancied himself something of a prophet. Abraham fancied him something of an eccentric but loved him deeply.

Rav Hillel pulled his white beard as he called, "Rabbi Cohen! Rabbi Cohen! Abraham!"

Abraham stretched and opened the office door. "I'm here, Rav," he said softly. "Shalom. Another bad dream you wish to share?"

Rav Hillel faced him and Abraham saw his brow painfully contorted, wrinkles even deeper than usual. "What is it?" Abraham asked.

Rav Hillel's eyes filled. His voice was low and raspy. "Deborah," he said. "Your wife."

"She is all right?" Abraham prompted.

Rav Hillel extended both his arms and lifted them, palms forward. For a moment, he stood very still, apparently summoning strength from the air. His eyes seemed to be only two more lines in his very lined face, his mouth threadlike. "Abraham," he breathed, "the baby."

"She has lost it," Abraham finished.

Rav Hillel bowed his head and lowered his hands. The two men walked silently out of the school and toward the hospital.

Autumn winds, pungent with the musk of decay, swept around them. Abraham's cheeks burned, and his eyes stung. He breathed in deeply and held the cold air that wanted to wail from his lungs and merge with the wind and pull more leaves from the trees.

Deborah was asleep in the hospital bed when the two

arrived. Her skin, next to the blue-white sheets, seemed ghostly, diaphanous. She had never been robust. Now she seemed a fragile china doll.

Abraham spoke her name. Her lips moved, but she did not open her eyes. He took her hand and sat on the chair by her bed. Rav Hillel left him there and promised to find a substitute for him at the school.

Abraham nodded and then bowed down to the bed. He put his head to his wife's empty womb and wept. Deborah looked at her husband and turned her head away.

"The Lord may try his people, but he will never forget them," Abraham said slowly.

Deborah nodded, and covered her face with her hands.

"Deborah."

She shook with silent sobs.

# CHAPTER 4

When Rabbi Cohen returned to school after three days' absence, Sarah saw one of the teachers talking to him, glancing accusingly at her as he spoke. She knew it would be a matter of minutes before the rabbi summoned her. She suspected it would be a brutal scolding this time. Perhaps (she dared not hope!) she would be expelled. She knew what the complaints against her would be and was ready with her defenses. Twenty minutes before the lunch hour, the rabbi called her. A couple of classmates gave her quick, significant looks. She rolled her eyes and shrugged.

Rabbi Cohen ushered her into his office, closed the door behind her, and sat at his desk.

Sarah grew flustered. She knew at once she could not offer her excuses, and she knew from looking at the rabbi that he would not be angry with her this day. He had been crying.

16

"Sarah," he said.

"Oh, Rabbi Cohen," she gushed, "why am I like I am? Is there something wrong with me? Am I defective? I don't mean to misbehave, but it just seems to happen, that's all. It just happens automatically."

"We all err. And so God has given us Yom Kippur, the Sabbath of Sabbaths, the Day of Atonement. Yom Kippur begins in three weeks."

"I know, Rabbi."

"For the transgressions between man and God, the Day of Atonement cleanses. But for the transgressions between man and his fellowman, atonement is effected only after the sinner has appeased the one against whom he has sinned."

"I know."

Rabbi Cohen nodded and seemed to struggle to remember what he was going to say. He brought his palm to his forehead and closed his eyes. "Once," he said, "a Gentile requested of the great Hillel to be taught Judaism while standing on one foot. Hillel's answer was, 'What you do not like yourself, do not do to others. The rest is commentary.' "

She nodded.

"And so, Sarah, it is a question not of obedience but of courtesy. Be kind to your teachers, for if you were in their position, you would want your students to be kind to you. Concern yourself with *shaliach mitzvah* — righteous deeds."

"Yes, Rabbi."

"Upon three things the world is based. Do you know what they are?"

She pursed her lips and stared at the ceiling. She could certainly guess one of the things. "The Torah."

"Yes. And what else?"

She stared again at the ceiling.

Rabbi Cohen saved her further embarrassment. "Upon three things the world is based: upon the Torah, upon divine service, and upon acts of loving kindness."

"Oh yes," she said.

He murmured, "Simon the Just," as he looked at some papers on his desk. Then, in a voice so low she had to crane her neck to hear, he went on. "Prepare yourself for Yom Kippur, Sarah. Prepare yourself by appeasing your teachers and by doing acts of loving kindness. That is all." He did not look at her, but she knew the *musar* was over. She had been dismissed.

"Thank you," she said meekly, and left.

But once outside the door, she had the urge to run back inside and confess a sin greater than the petty grievances the teachers had brought against her. In fact, she had sinned terribly. She had gone for a walk last Sunday and somehow found herself in the vicinity of the American Christian church, the church of the missionaries who had prayed outside her door, The Church of Jesus Christ of Latter-day Saints. She had entered. And that was not all. She, a Jew, had fallen in love with one of the boys in the meeting. Yes, with a Christian.

She glanced towards the office again, almost ready to confess. Rabbi Cohen had his face in his hands. Sarah turned away and went back to class.


The boy had watched her steadily during that church meeting. But whenever her eyes had drifted to his, he had turned away. After the meeting, she had found him (his white hair glistened like a halo), approached him, and introduced herself. "You look familiar," she had said. "I'm wondering — were we in school together?"

"You look familiar too," he replied. His voice was a mild

tenor. "I was sure when I saw you here today that I had seen you before. You were in Mrs. Veinsinger's class, weren't you? The younger class?"

"And—and you were in Mrs. Wobbe's," she said, remembering him from the years she had attended a public school, calculating his age to be three years older than hers. "I heard Mrs. Wobbe was a witch."

"Yes, she was."

They talked more about the school, until the boy abruptly said, "You're Jewish, aren't you? Why are you here?"

"Well," she hesitated, "your missionaries came to our house. They had a message and said it was for Jews and Gen—" she caught herself. "Non-Jews."

"Then you're investigating the Church."

"Yes, that's right."

"Wonderful! If I can be of any help, please—I can teach you, if you want, all about it." He straightened himself. "I plan on being a missionary myself."

"I would like that very much," she said.

The boy—he said his name was Hans Grubbe—introduced her to his sour-looking, sixteen-year-old sister, Gertrude, who took hold of his elbow and smiled at Sarah. Even the smile was sour, almost painful. And when she spoke in her tiny voice, she seemed quite out of breath. "So glad to meet you," she said.

Sarah shook her hand and repeated, "Glad to meet you."

Hans asked where she lived. Sarah told him. "It's on our way," he said, then turned to his sister. "Well, Gerti, shall we walk our new friend home? She's investigating the Church."

Gertrude stretched her smile.

As they walked, Hans told Sarah a few things about the Church and promised to contact her soon to arrange for "lessons." He and Gertrude both shook her hand at her door, and Sarah went inside, wearing a stupid grin. Her father asked where she had been. She murmured, "With friends."

Every day thereafter, including the day of Rabbi Cohen's scolding, Sarah had dashed home from school, wanting Hans to be waiting for her by the front door. Whenever she caught a glimpse of blonde hair, her stomach tightened. Even on the day the rabbi reprimanded her, Sarah ran the last block to her house, and flushed when she saw a blond boy waiting by the door. But as she approached, she saw that it was not Hans but the mail carrier, who had lovely hair but rotten teeth and cratered skin. He was delivering a letter to David from some Jewish political organization.

By the end of Yom Kippur, Hans still had not come. Sarah flirted with the thought that God was guiding her away from the boy and his faith, but it seemed much more logical that Hans was simply too busy with his studies to come, or too shy. And, of course, there was always the possibility that he had come and been turned away by an overprotective family member. She did not broach the subject with David. David's piety sometimes took explosive turns.

After a month, Sarah went again to the "Mormon" church, which was just dismissing. She saw Hans, standing by an autumn-rusted oak tree, leaning on crutches, his left leg heavily bandaged.

She waved as soon as he noticed her. He lifted one crutch in response.

"Now I understand why you didn't come to teach me about your church," she said dramatically, running up to him. "How did you hurt your leg?"

"A hole in the ground."

"Perhaps you could teach me now?"

"Now?"

"If you want to. You could begin anyway."

Hans looked around and then shrugged. "All right," he said. "You've heard the Joseph Smith story, I guess."

"No, not really."

"Well," he said, "Joseph Smith—about a hundred years ago in America—God called him as a prophet. The prophet of the Restoration."

"Prophet? Like Moses?"

Hans smiled. "Exactly."

"Like Moses," she repeated.

"Joseph Smith saw God and Jesus and was told that he would be permitted to restore the true church with all its doctrines and powers and ordinances. Anyway, later on, Joseph Smith saw an angel who told him about some ancient records he was to find and translate by the gift and power of God."

Sarah made her eyes go very big to show how well she was listening and how well she was impressed and how pretty her eyes were.

"So anyway, the book is the Book of Mormon. You have a copy, don't you? If not, I'll lend you mine."

"I'd love to read yours," she said.

With his crutch, he motioned to a small case by his bandaged foot. She opened it and found a leather-bound, black book. On its cover was a golden man blowing a long-necked, golden trumpet. "Is this it?" she asked, knowing very well it was, for its title was boldly lettered.

Hans nodded.

"For how long may I borrow it?" she asked, hoping he would set a short limit.

"Until you're finished. I'll try to get over to your place sometime, but it's hard, you know, with my leg like this." He motioned with his chin to the bandages. "So if you come to church again next Sunday, we can talk about it then."

Sarah gave her most glamorous smile.

# CHAPTER 5

Hans did not visit her during the week, but Sarah secretly read the Book of Mormon every night. The book was very interesting in some parts and very boring in others. She didn't understand much of it, but what she did understand seemed sophisticated enough to be true. At least it was hard enough to read. By Sunday, she had read through the book of Enos — a formidable amount, she thought. She told her father she was going to visit friends and then went to the Mormon church.

"Well," said Hans when they met after Sunday School, "did you get a chance to read the Book of Mormon?"

"I've read through Enos," she announced.

"Good. And what do you think?"

"I think it would be wonderful to hear voices from Heaven and see angels and visions like that."

They walked outside the church to the oak tree. Its branches were bare save five rusty leaves and one withered gray one.

Hans leaned against the tree. "You and I are a lot alike. I've thought the same things," he said.

"Do you think it's possible to have such experiences? I mean for someone like—for people like us?"

When she raised her face to his, he was looking at her with an intensity she had seen only in David's eyes. It seemed to bore into her brain and brand her soul with his answer: "Yes!"

"Yes?" she repeated weakly.

"Yes! I really believe that. That's why I want to be a missionary."

Sarah was about to ask him if missionaries could be married, when Gertrude joined them. Conversation lightened, and Hans and his sister walked her home.


She finished the Book of Mormon in four months and had occasional conversations with Hans about its contents. When she read Third Nephi, she was struck by the thought that if the book were true, Jesus was the Messiah. And if that were true, the Mormon church was His church—the church of the Messiah. And if that were so, she was justified in loving Hans and in visiting his church, regardless of what Rabbi Cohen might think.

The thought that the Mormon church might be true did not overwhelm her. Matters of religion had never concerned her except when they had interfered with her home life. More important than religion to Sarah was love. And she loved Hans.

She decided shortly after Chanukah that she would be baptized into the Mormon church. This would mean, she surmised happily, that she would be expelled from the Hilde

Goldstein Beth Yacov School for Girls. Then she would not have to fear the rabbi.

Being underage, she would have to have her parents' written consent in order to be baptized, the branch president advised her, but she saw no problem with that. She was certain her father would be more than willing to let his daughter join another church. What did he care? He didn't live his parents' faith. And her mother, after a couple days of crying and threatening, would sullenly relent as well. David would consider it a personal affront—which didn't bother her in the least.

She approached her father in the evening, after supper. He was reading a book and looking very comfortable lying on the floor. His head was propped up by three pillows. She knelt beside him.

"Papa," she said, "I need to talk to you."

Aaron Sinasohn wore thick, round, wire-framed glasses when he read. These he now pushed down his nose until they almost touched his mustache. He raised his eyes to her.

"You know," she said, picking a piece of lint from his sweater, "there is something I must confess to you."

"Perhaps about your visiting the American church? Yes?"

"How did you know?"

"Customers tell me. Your mother, of course, she wanted me to talk to you about it, but I said, 'Sarah's nearly fourteen years old. Some girls her age—very poor ones—they're getting married already. Our daughter needs to explore things,' I told her. 'Let her see what is outside, and then her decisions will be meaningful to her.' But we knew about it. When we went for our walks with Moses, sometimes we waited at the corner to see if you would leave. Sometimes I followed you, to make sure no harm came your way."

"It's not far."

"I know. And anyway, it is your life, and you will make your own decisions. Isn't that right?"

"And that's what I want to talk to you about. My decision. I want to join the Mormon church."

"You want to join it?" he said, clearing his throat. "Why?"

"Why?" she repeated. "Why? Because—because I like it."

"The church, or that tall boy I see you talk to sometimes? Which is it really that you like? Which?"

"You've seen me with Hans?"

"Is that his name? A good, German name, for a member of an American church."

"It's nothing serious."

"Changing religion is nothing serious?"

"Not that, but—"

"Nothing serious?" he repeated, his voice going into its hoarse, upper registers the way it did when he and David argued. "Now, I am no zaddik—the Almighty knows 'Aaron the Jew' stinks of trefa—but it is one thing to relax with regard to one's religion. It is another thing entirely to forsake one's religion."

"I said nothing about forsaking my religion, only about joining another church."

Aaron fell back on his pillows and laughed. Then he sighed deeply. "I know you hear me fight with David about matters of our faith," he said slowly. "Conflicts of belief. Well, those are family issues, aren't they? But, Sarah, the truth is, the other churches hate us. They love us only if we forsake our faith and accept theirs. Your friends, even that handsome boy, they would leave you forever if you told them you would not change from being a Jew."

"No they wouldn't."

"They would, I tell you. They would!"

"It is still my decision, whether I join the American church or not, isn't it?"

"Yes. Yes, it is. And when you are of age, you can make that decision. But now, on this night, I, your father, forbid it. You tell your friends you will not wear a cross around your neck. And if they still accept you, then we will talk." He pushed his glasses back to his eyes and opened his book again.

For a long time, Sarah stayed beside him, her eyes filling with tears. She swallowed and wiped her cheeks. "What if," she whined, "what if I believed in the other church?"

"Then that would be a different matter," he said, and turned a page.

Sarah went to her room. Hans's Book of Mormon was under her bed. She retrieved it and sluggishly asked, "Well, is your church true?"

As she expected would be the case, nothing happened. No voices. No lights. No trumpeting.

Sarah lay on her bed and thought about her future. It seemed that her life could be only empty longing were Hans not in its center. And she knew that if she were not a Mormon, Hans could never be hers. She wanted Hans more than she had ever wanted anything.

For two weeks, she didn't go to the Mormon church. When again she ventured inside it, on an icy day, Hans was sitting at the sacrament table.

"If God is love," she told herself, "then this church is God's. For me it is, anyway."

Hans and Gertrude walked her home again after the meetings.

When they stood at the Sinasohn porch, Sarah said, "I believe in the Mormon church. I am going to ask my father for permission to be baptized."

Gertrude hugged her. Hans smiled and shook her hand. She felt that she had already completed a rite of passage, though the harshest initiatory test was sitting comfortably before the fireplace inside. (She decided not to mention her father's already stated disapproval to the Grubbes.) Hans and Gertrude wished her Heaven's blessings and left.

Sarah breathed in the frosty air. It stung her lungs. She pulled her scarf tightly around her head and neck and plunged her hands into her coat pockets. For a moment, she stood shivering, alone on the porch, watching her Christian friends fade into the winter scene. She reached for the doorknob and then moved away. She was not ready yet for the confrontation. She tried to catch a last glimpse of Gertrude and Hans, but all she could see were icy trees and mother-of-pearl clouds.

One tree, a young willow, was coated with a film of silvery, shining ice, which reflected the last gold of the setting sun. The tree was an inverted chandelier. It seemed to be speaking to her, telling her some secrets about life and faith and eternity and mortality. It was utterly naked and frozen, but still alive. Beneath the ice was life. It spoke of the future, of chandeliered dances, and it spoke of other, more abstract things: cold things, dead things, which she could not understand. The tree was death, but it was also the shining bush on Sinai, and God was hiding under its ice. It was Messiah, with promises of victory over the winter of the Jews. It was Jesus Christ. It was the Tree of Life. Her tears came once more and she told the tree fervently, "I really do believe." The brittle branches swayed as though rehearsing the movements of spring. "I do believe," she repeated.

She returned to the front door, hesitated, then entered. Her father did not even open his eyes when she came in, but asked, "And how are the Mormons today?"

"I believe in their church," she announced. "Please, please let me join it."

Aaron yawned.

"I want it more than anything."

"You used to want chocolate more than anything," he said, his lips curving into an amused smile.

Sarah rushed to the chair where he was sitting, knelt by it and said, "Everything else in my life imitates happiness. The Mormon church is—"

Aaron coughed and opened one eye. "Please, Sarah. You sound like a girl leaving a Rudolph Valentino movie. Please, please. I know about all of that. No one escapes life without a few days of longing for religion, you know. Longing to know all the answers, or at least to be a part of a group which claims to know them all. Longing to be reassured of immortality so that life's drudgery may be endured. Oh, I know. I've lived with David, haven't I? I recognize all the signs of religious desperation. Let us not be melodramatic, though." He opened the other eye.

"May I be baptized into their church?"

He twitched his mouth and stroked his mustache. "I don't understand," he said at last, "how I, who am, God knows, relaxed in my faith, have managed to produce two religious zealots. Or perhaps I have just answered my own question. Perhaps if I had been more religious, you and David would have had your fill, yes? It must be a human need to worship. A human necessity. And of course, Christianity offers more hope than Judaism, because the Christian Messiah has already come, is already saving souls, isn't that right? It is tantalizing, isn't it? Yes, I can see that. But this does not change the fact that, despite all appearances, Sarah, we are Jews. Judaism is sculpted into your body. Yes, Sarah! Your nose, your eyes, your complexion all say that you are a Jew. Even your name—of course, your mother chose that. Nonetheless, you must understand that Judaism is not just candles in a menorah."

"Then I shall be a Mormon Jew," she answered.

"A what?"

"A Mormon Jew. I can be a Mormon and a Jew together."

"You think so?" Aaron sighed. "You and your mother," he chuckled. "So alike! May your husband be blessed! And patient."

Sarah spoke plainly now. "You are avoiding the issue. May I join the Mormon church?"

"Why don't you ask David?"

"David!" She raised her hands. "Maybe I won't ask anyone. Maybe I will just go and join the church and no one will be the wiser."

"My customers would tell me, wouldn't they?"

"It would be too late by the time they did."

"Maybe not."

Her knees began to ache. She stood and paced. "Christianity is really just a part of Judaism, you know."

"As a fluke is a part of a sheep."

"Jesus was a Jew."

"Sarah, I'm tired," complained Aaron.

"I'm tired too! Tired of you always telling me that you expect me to be grown-up and independent and proper—and then standing in my way when I make my own decisions."

"You think I would not stand in your way if you wanted to jump off a cliff?"

"I don't want to jump off a cliff. I'm not as stupid as you seem to think."

"Or if you wanted to tear my left arm off?"

"I don't want to—"

"And the right arm off your mother? Sarah, think for a moment, think of what this would do to your mother. Think!"

"I can't live my life just to please my mother."

"That's true. But there are plenty of criminals in jails who said the same thing once, isn't that so?"

"Joining a church is not quite like robbing a bank."

"Doing one thing which makes your mother weep is not entirely different from doing another thing which makes her weep. The tears are the same; they fall down the same cheeks."

"Now you're being melodramatic."

He made a quick, angry gesture and then put his hand to his mouth and chuckled again. "And you're just like me. May your husband be blessed, and may he be strong." He leveled his finger at her. "Stronger than you!"

"You're still evading the issue."

"You're still a child."

"You told me that it was good to explore. That I should learn about other religions so I could make my own decisions. If you really believed in Judaism—but you don't! You eat *trefa*. You fight with David when he wants you to go to the synagogue. You bring home crab."

"Why don't you get on one side of me and put David on the other and both of you have a tug-of-war?"

"You don't like people controlling your life any more than I do. And here you are, playing the proper papa and acting like you don't understand. And you still haven't answered the question. You said if I really believed in the Mormon church . . . "

Suddenly Aaron shouted, "All right!" His words filled the room. Then he spoke softly and low. "If you insist on doing this thing, you do it. But afterwards, I want to hear nothing more about it. You will find out enough on your own, if you're so determined. Only do not murder the Jews, your family. 'Honor thy father and thy mother . . .' "

"Mormons believe in the Torah too," she said lamely.

"I give you my blessing," he said and closed his eyes. "I hope it doesn't kill your mother."

"Thank you." She murmured the words like an epithet.

Dinner that night was served and eaten in silence. David and Frau Eva Sinasohn took turns glaring at Aaron and at Sarah.

Moses asked innocently, "Is something wrong?" and was told, "Eat, eat, and be a good boy."

Sarah asked Hans to baptize her. His mother, Frau Grubbe, made her a simple, white tunic for the occasion. Sarah felt like a bride in it.

The water of the river was half frozen. She shivered as Hans led her into it. Somehow, the cold did not affect him. He smiled and took her hand, pronounced the prayer, then immersed her and brought her up quickly again.

On the bank, the branch president's wife wrapped her in a quilt and gave a wool blanket to Hans. An old man, who, Sarah was told, had been the first member of the Church in Hamburg, confirmed her and gave her the gift of the Holy Ghost.

Afterwards, they all went to the branch president's house, where pastry and fruit juice were served.

Sarah could not keep from looking at Hans. They had both grown up considerably since their first meeting. Indeed, she was womanly now. She was the age Joseph Smith had been when he had received his first vision. Surely the Lord considered a person of fourteen to be an adult. David had become

Bar Mitzvah when he turned thirteen, as was the Jewish custom. David's whole life had changed then. Her whole family had changed then.

She was reminded of David's piety when she returned home after her baptism. David quivered and looked as though he were restraining himself from attacking her. "Did you?" he asked.

The ends of her hair were still damp. She answered easily, "Of course."

"There are people in Germany, you know, who want to slaughter the Jews." His voice trembled.

She glanced at him, rolled her eyes, and went to her room. There she wrote a love letter to Hans. She would show it to him, she told herself, after they were married.

# CHAPTER 6

David did not eat with the family that night or the next. When he came to the table after three days of hardly an appearance within the home, he was visibly thinner and pale. Sarah could not bring herself to look at him.

As Eva Sinasohn cleared the table, David addressed his father. "What do you think of that man Adolf Hitler?"

Aaron coughed and shook his head. "I've heard stories. Nothing I care to believe."

"Oh, the stories are real. Hitler wants to be chancellor. And he would slaughter the Jews if he could."

Aaron coughed again. "Plenty of anti-Semites in the world and in Germany—I don't have to tell you that. But what good does this fretting do? Hate consumes itself, doesn't it? Am I right? I don't suppose that's in our scriptures, but it should be. Hate consumes itself. Those who hate become cannibals. Eat their own bodies. That should be in our scriptures too."

"It is. Well, at least similar thoughts. Rabbi Eliazar said—"

"Please, David, I don't care to hear what Rabbi Eliazar said. Not at the dinner table."

"Or anywhere else, for that matter," David murmured. "All right, then; fine. We'll use your analogy. Don't you think one who finally eats his own flesh has first developed an appetite by tasting the flesh of other humans—the first victims of his hate, let us say?"

"You are the devout Jew in this family, David. Do you think God would permit an anti-Semite to kill his chosen people?"

"If God controlled the devil, God could be blamed for the destruction of Jerusalem and the Temple," David said.

"That's true, I suppose." Aaron nodded thoughtfully. "So you say God will let Hitler become chancellor if the Germans want it?"

"Yes."

"All right. Then I will begin to be afraid on the day this Hitler takes office. Until then, I have other things on my mind. I will not worry until then, you hear me?"

"I hear. And while you wait—while you lounge in your apathy—I will prepare. Hitler wants to blame us for the Kaiser's fall. Did you know that?"

"Oh, I'm certain he does. You think he's the only one who wants to do that? Well? Only Hitler? And how would you have me respond to these crazies? What should I do? Tell me— what? Cower in the corner of my house? Let my bakery rot?"

"Pray to God for our protection. Pray with me. I want you to go with me to the synagogue for morning prayers."

"Well, this is new," Aaron said, chuckling. "And very interesting. So it is really a matter of prayer. This is what you are suggesting?"

"Yes. Prayer. And God hasn't heard your prayers for a very long time."

"What you're saying is that if enough people pray to God for protection, the devil will be defeated, yes? But if more people pray for our destruction, well—then the devil wins. Very interesting." He raised his brows, stroked his mustache pensively. "Is that in our scriptures too? Did I overlook that at the yeshiva when I was a boy?"

"Papa—" David said, motioning vaguely to Sarah. "Please, let's not argue. Especially—"

"But you see—" Aaron began, then stopped. He looked at David, who was staring sadly into space. "The Egyptians must have prayed to their gods for victory," Aaron said after a moment. "And when the angels danced to celebrate the demise of the Hebrews' enemies, God would not let them. 'The Egyptians are my children, too,' God said. 'Be reverent.' "

David nodded.

"But I must disagree with one thing you imply," Aaron went on. "We may not be controlled by God, but neither are we controlled by Satan. Between light and darkness is dawn and dusk. Yes? Am I not right? And there—there is man. Such words! Such words of wisdom should be in our scriptures, too." His voice danced. "Man is free until he chooses one side or the other. And so prayers, David, can only be pleas of men who have already selected their alliances. No man can pray to destroy another soul, only to know more of God."

"Then there could not be a chosen people," said David, glancing furtively at Sarah.

Aaron leaned back in his chair. "Would you agree that God chooses those who choose him? He has destroyed Jews as well as Gentiles, has he not? *If* the words of Moses are factual."

"Of course they're factual."

"And a convert to Judaism is as though born under the covenant."

David opened his mouth to reply, but it was Sarah who spoke. "Perhaps," she said, "all things are spiritual to God."

The father and son stared at her incredulously. They were used to private debates — certainly without interruptions from the women of the family, and absolutely without interruptions from the children.

"What do you mean, daughter?" asked Aaron, frowning.

"I was thinking, maybe man makes history, but God uses it to teach spiritual lessons. That's what I was thinking," she said.

Aaron considered the idea with a deeper frown and then shrugged. David only stared at her. His eyes made her giggle. She said no more, and the discussion changed to news of the neighborhood.


As she lay in bed that night, Sarah thought about the dinner-time conversation. Her conversion to Mormonism had changed her; she saw that clearly now. The whole perspective of her life had shifted. She thought of David and her father. She was no longer a part of her own family. They did not accept her. She did not fit in. Her tears dropped down her cheeks and collected around her ears. When she finally slept, she dreamed of spring flowers, lush meadows, and Hans.

Outside, the winter wind howled as though stirred up by demons.

On October 31 that same year, Adolf Hitler was received by Field Marshal Paul von Hindenburg, president of Germany.

# C H A P T E R  7

Hitler took office as chancellor of Germany on January 30, 1933.

Within a few months, through terror, violence, and the innovation of concentration camps, Hitler suppressed all political parties, the trade-union movement, the free press, the political institutions of the Weimar Republic. Always, he was obsessed with the concept of international Jewry and Bolshevism.

"There are only two possibilities in Germany," he had said in 1922, "either victory of the Aryan or annihilation of the Aryan and the victory of the Jew."

Hitler's henchmen, initially called the "SA," sang polkas about "Jew blood spurting from the knife." They spread such lies as had long ago been spread about the Talmud and *Shulhan Aruch* commanding Jews to deceive, rob, and kill non-Jews.

Of course, anti-Semitism was nothing new in Europe. It was, in fact, a long-standing tradition. But Jews in Germany had reached equality under the law. The Weimar Republic, established after the first World War, had abolished all their previous restrictions of law and status. Indeed, the Jews considered themselves authentically German. One hundred thousand of them had served in the German forces in World War I; twelve thousand had died in battle. There had even been a Jewish foreign minister after the war. And so, to most German Jews, the lies and efforts to denigrate or boycott them seemed offensive but childish. Hitler simply was not taken seriously by much of the Semitic population.

Even after his associate Goering set up the first concentration camp in Sachsenhausen in 1933, Hitler's true goals and power to carry them out seemed no more probable than the lies of the SA.

To Aaron, Hitler was a laughable buffoon.

Rav Hillel, of course, predicted a holocaust and headed a group of young Jewish politicians.

David Sinasohn became a member of that group.


David went to Rav Hillel's apartment every Wednesday night. He never spoke about what happened there, but the Sinasohns knew he was involved in political planning. One Wednesday Aaron teased him about going to the "Subterfuge Party." David answered, "If you will not pray with me—even now—then you will not judge my efforts to keep us safe. You have no right!"

Aaron chuckled, but Sarah sensed discomfort behind his laugh.

One Thursday, David came to supper wearing a silly, sickly smile. Between bites, he talked about Joseph of Egypt. He told the whole story, from the coat of many colors to the reunion of the sons of Jacob, and talked about how the Jewish nation would be as Joseph, despite this man Hitler.

As David spoke, Sarah saw him as Joseph: regal, serious, serene, encircled by prostrate, faceless brothers who did not recognize him. In her imagination, David as Joseph went to another room and wept, then returned and spoke, not in Egyptian as he had heretofore done, but in Hebrew. "Brothers, I am Joseph."

How could Joseph's own brothers have failed to recognize him? Time could not have changed him so much. It must have been only that they had not expected to find him thus. They had not expected their own foolish brother to be sitting on a throne. They had not expected him to be their savior.

"And we too will surprise our oppressors," David was saying. Aaron complimented him on his storytelling talent and then talked about separatism and the Haskalah movement. A half-friendly debate developed, which Sarah tuned out. She was still thinking of Joseph.

"Brothers. Brothers, it is I. Joseph." But she was not thinking of Joseph only. She was thinking of Jesus, another savior who had been rejected by his brothers.

"What would you think about having a daughter-in-law?" David said.

Sarah was jolted from her dreams. "What?" she said.

Aaron, shaking his head slowly, chuckled and then laughed with his son, laughed hard. "I thought there might be something like that on your mind. Maybe you do more than politics on Wednesdays, eh? A little bit more? Well, what's her name?"

David resumed his silly grinning and told the family about

another member of Rav Hillel's group: a girl named Zipporah Steinberg. Zippi.

The next week, he brought her home.

She was a tall, bushy-haired girl with stark features and a pointed chin. Sarah privately dubbed her "Amazon Queen." She was stately, dark, and quite plain. Nonetheless, God granted a miracle, and when Zippi and David were married one month later, Zippi actually looked nice.

David wore his brown suit and smiled broadly at the wedding guests. He was the radiant one. Zippi was serene and not nearly as homely as usual. But David beamed.

During the reading of the *Ketubah*, David resumed his familiar seriousness. During the ceremony, he was intense. His face puckered with concentration as Rabbi Cohen recited the seven benedictions.

Together the bride and groom stood under the canopy. David slipped a gold band onto Zippi's finger at the appointed time, shared a sip of wine with her, and stamped on the glass chalice from which they had drunk. This breaking of the glass was done in remembrance of the ancient temple's destruction. The crowd burst into a resounding, *"Mazel tov!"* and David's intense face moved into joy. Zippi smiled serenely. The dancing began.

Sarah thought of Hans during the wedding, fantasized about being his bride. Of course, she was too young to marry yet, but time was marching. Hans was going away to France within the month, to a university in Paris. By the time he graduated, she would be of marriageable age.

She looked at the newlyweds, dancing with partners other than each other but exchanging glances. There was something miraculous about the entire scene. David was exultant; his smile filled the room. It seemed that his piety had finally paid off.

And homely Zippi was transformed by her love. The room itself seemed to sway with euphoria. Laughter, song, and dancing celebrated the union of the man and woman, and, simultaneously, the covenant between God and Israel.

Of course, Sarah thought, hers would be a Mormon wedding. When she and Hans married—and there she stopped.

Her marriage to Hans was not a certain thing. She was not even sure how he felt about her. Sometimes he seemed to look at her tenderly, but other times—and especially recently—he seemed hard, distant, opaque.

On the surface, nothing had changed between her and Hans, but nothing had happened either. They still usually met together on Sundays after sacrament meeting, and he and Gertrude usually walked her home. But he never visited her during the week. He never tried to hold her hand. She did not know what he felt for her.

Someone grabbed her by the elbow and urged her to participate in the circle dances. She acquiesced and joined the celebrants, finding herself opposite Rabbi Cohen and his wife.

The rabbi knew of her Mormonism, of course, though he had not confronted her with it as she had expected him to. (Several of her classmates had refused to talk to her after the rumors of her conversion spread.) Nor had she been expelled from the school, as she had hoped she might be, though her parents did let her attend a public school after the year ended. But, though she had not seen the rabbi in a long time and he had never openly condemned her, she could not bear his sad gaze. After the dancing, she left the synagogue quickly.

# CHAPTER 8

Hans told Sarah the next Sunday that he was scheduled to take a train to Paris in the morning.

She was simply stunned. She had known he would be leaving, but not so soon. Her mouth dropped as she tried to make it smile. She blinked against rising tears. "I'll walk you home," he offered.

She nodded vaguely and looked for Gertrude, who was nowhere to be seen.

It was a hot day, but Sarah had worn a sweater in the morning and hadn't bothered to take it off. She didn't remove it now, either, because it had pockets in which she kept her hands, fists clenching and unclenching as though holding the torn halves of her heart. She said nothing.

When they turned up her street, Hans said, "You will keep going to church, I hope, even though I won't be there."

She wasn't sure just what he meant, but he sounded suspicious. "Of course," she answered.

"The Church needs you, you know."

"Does it?"

"You have some good qualities," he said.

"Do I?"

"Yes."

"What?"

He looked at her with a half smile. "Well," he said, "you're bright. You're sensitive. You're curious. You're brave."

"Am I all those things?"

"Many good qualities," he repeated.

"I appreciate your influence," she said. "You were the one who got me to read the Book of Mormon, you know. Actually, it was your book. You'll always be—always—significant—to me for that." Her cheeks burned; the moisture in her mouth seemed consumed by the heat.

"And you to me," he said, looking away. "You were the first person I baptized."

She glanced at the willow tree—her Tree of Life—and at the setting sun descending to the horizon on apricot clouds. Night would take the color from the sky and replace the clouds with constellations. In the morning, Hans would be gone.

"I will miss you," she said. As soon as the words were spoken, her face crumpled with emotion. She covered it with one sprawled hand and sobbed, "I'm sorry. I didn't mean to cry—I didn't mean—I feel so stupid."

Hans touched her hair. "It's all right," he said. "I'll be back soon."

She nodded jerkily, and sobbed again.

With a sigh, Hans put his arm around her. "Shhh," he breathed. "Hush, you silly girl."

Again, she made an effort to quiet herself. It failed. Her breast heaved and shook.

"Hush, Sarah," he said, and gently kissed her cheek.

That stopped her crying at once.

Hans had kissed her!

She took a deep breath, dropped the hand that had covered her face, and reverently said, "Hans, I love you."

Now he blushed, and looked at her with shock. He stammered, "You do?"

Sarah's eyes brimmed again, not from love this time but embarrassment. She understood now. Hans had never regarded her as more than a child or a potential convert. She was, as it were, his donation to the Church, the first statistic of his missionary career. She was corban, like any other tithe or offering: valued for its "good qualities," as is a chicken for its eggs, but not loved. Not loved the way she loved him. Not thought of even as human. And why? There could be but one explanation: she was a Jew. Her father had been right.

She stepped away. "I know you hate me," she said in a voice even softer than the one which had declared her love.

He shook his head.

"You've been cold towards me for months. You talk with your head, not your heart."

"That's not true," he said.

"Isn't it? Then tell me why you are so cold to me all the time?"

Hans's jaw was taut. When he spoke, his voice was quiet but defiant. "You know the answer to that."

"I do not."

"Yes, you do. Don't make me say it."

"Why do I make you so nervous? Are you scared of being seen with a Jew?"

"What? No!"

"It doesn't matter."

"It does matter. I don't hate you, Sarah, and you know that. How would you feel, tell me, if you were a seventeen-year-old boy and you had managed—somehow—to fall in love with a child? And a Jew at that! Not that it matters to me. But would you want her—want anyone—to know? Sarah!"

"You love me?"

He took her hand tentatively. They walked further, away from the Sinasohn home towards the rustle of a little waterfall in a nearby glen. A bridge that had once been bright red but was now faded and termite eaten hunched over the stream and creaked at their steps. Hans was silent, almost awkward. He and Sarah watched dragonflies flit around mossy stones. They breathed in the pine scents, listened to the rush of water. "I have never in my life seen such beauty as this," sighed Sarah.

Hans nodded.

"Paradise should be no lovelier."

He shut his eyes.

"Hans," she said.

He looked at her nervously.

"I want you to hold me."

Stiffly, he touched her shoulders and leaned towards her. She embraced him gently, then backed away. "I love you," she repeated.

"I love you," he said, pausing between each word.

They began walking to her home again.


Hans wrote often to Sarah from the university. She wrote to him even more frequently, and she sealed each letter with an invisible kiss.

# C H A P T E R  9

In November 1934, Sarah turned sixteen. Some fuss was made over her, a small party given, but nothing compared with the fuss made over Moses on October 21, 1935, when he turned thirteen. It was time for him to become Bar Mitzvah—a son of the commandment. David had tutored him in preparation for the ceremony.

Sarah, as a Mormon, felt awkward venturing inside the synagogue for Moses' Bar Mitzvah. But Eva Sinasohn would not hear of her missing the event. It seemed as important to Eva to have Sarah present as Moses. Sarah suspected that there were other motives than family unity.

Rabbi Abraham Cohen was standing before the congregation as Sarah made her way to the women's section. It was he who would call Moses up to recite the prayers of thanksgiving for the Torah. Sarah tensed.

Moses, his oversized glasses magnifying his eyes, sat between David and Aaron. He looked serious and devout but
very little. When he was called up to recite the blessings, his
gangly legs seemed to give way under him. He stumbled but
quickly recovered and faced the congregation. His recitation
was not only flawless but poignant. He seemed to be pro-
nouncing his blessing much as a groom recites the scripted
vows — as though inventing the words spontaneously from his
own heart and soul. He licked his lips nervously as he finished
the recitation and gave a shy smile to the audience.

Sarah, feeling that she was peeking into a familiar home
which had once been hers but now belonged to someone else,
could not help but feel proud of her skinny little brother.

Rabbi Cohen began to speak. After two years, he still affected her. She wanted to leave the synagogue quickly to avoid
a confrontation.

When the rituals were ended, she hurriedly congratulated
her brother, pretended not to hear the kiddush, and turned
to leave. Rabbi Cohen's familiar voice called her back. She
turned to face him.

He looked more mild and gentle than ever she had seen
him. He said softly, "Hello, Sarah. I'm sure you're proud of
your brother today."

She nodded once, perfunctorily. "Certainly so."

"He is a good boy."

"Yes." She glanced at the rabbi's face and then away.

"This is a big step in his life."

"A big step."

"And how are you?" His rich voice, his soft smile under-
scored her embarrassment.

"I'm fine, Rabbi Cohen," she said.

She wanted to tell him about Hans, about that night when

she had felt with her soul that Jesus was Messiah, about Joseph of Egypt, about her tree. She wanted him to know that she had not become a Mormon to spite her family or him, or out of fear of Hitler, but that she believed in her new religion. All she could manage as a synopsis of these details was a fervent repetition of the words she had just spoken. "I'm fine. I'm fine," she said, looking him in the eye.

"I am so glad to hear it."

She bowed her head. "Thank you for everything. This day meant so much to my brother, and you were an important part of it."

"My dear Sarah, you are very welcome." He walked slowly away and joined his wife, Deborah, by the door of the synagogue. He said something to her that Sarah could not hear. But she could guess the message, for Deborah looked at her soulfully.

The next Tuesday afternoon, the rabbi's wife called on her.


Deborah Cohen epitomized the righteous, ever-patient woman of Israel. She was gentle, graceful, purposeful in all her movements, and likewise in her conversations. And so she got to the point quickly. "Israel has been plagued by many false messiahs," she said.

Sarah took a deep breath.

"It would be a shame, wouldn't it, to follow a lovely bird to a slippery precipice?" Her voice seemed never above a whisper.

Sarah nodded.

"And today, more than ever, Judah needs his daughters to gather and be strong."

Half reclined on the sofa, Sarah did not reply. Deborah

returned her mute stare and then continued, as naturally as if
the confrontation had been choreographed. "You know, Sarah,
Israel is the suffering servant of God, and Israel has suffered
more under the whips and rumors of the Christians than ever
it suffered under the pharaohs. Don't you see? That is why we
cannot afford to lose any of our number to our persecutors.
Then they are strengthened and we—you understand, don't
you?" Her brow was furrowed in a network of tiny wrinkles.

Sarah sat up straighter. "The Christians have been perse-
cuted, too," she said.

"Yes. Before the time of Constantine. But, dear Sarah, don't
you see? At that time, the Christians were a small sect of Jews.
Now Christianity embraces the world and the world returns
the embrace. And smothers us between."

"Yes. I can see that." She did not want to look into the
woman's golden eyes.

Deborah took Sarah's hand. "We need you back with us,
dear."

She did not answer.

"It's very hard for you, isn't it?"

"I didn't join the Mormon church to hurt anyone. I did it
because I believed in it. Why can't people just leave me alone
and let me live my life?"

"How old are you, Sarah?"

"I turned sixteen in November."

"And you feel you are old enough to make all your own
decisions? Yes, I suppose you do. I did too when I was sixteen.
But, oh my dear, the world is so full of slander, so full of
deception, so full of hate—you will see. Believe me. You will
see."

"Perhaps I will."

Deborah's cheeks glowed like pearls when she smiled. "I

don't want to control your life, Sarah. I know how frustrating it is to have someone else interfere with your decisions. Just know that if you ever should want to return to us, we will receive you with open arms. We miss you, Sarah. We want you back. There, now I've said it. I won't say anything else. God bless you, my dear."

Sarah nodded again, tried to smile, timidly murmured, "Thank you." She felt Deborah's quick kiss on her cheek and waited, head bowed, until she heard the front door open and close.

# CHAPTER 10

Germany's changes continued. Its economy was stabilizing. New factories were opening up. But hand-in-hand with economic progress went new laws restricting Jews from government, from institutions of higher learning, and, in 1935, from intermarriage with Aryans. Already existing marriages in violation of this law were declared void. Extramarital relations between German citizens and Jews were prohibited. Jews were restricted from hiring female Germans under forty-five years of age as housekeepers and were not allowed to display the national colors.

On November 14, 1935, Jews were defined in three degrees: (1) full-blooded, or having three or more racially full Jewish grandparents, or a person belonging to the Jewish religious community; (2) "*Mischling*, first degree," or having two Jewish grandparents; and (3) "*Mischling*, second degree," or having one Jewish grandparent.

Sarah, of course, was a full Jew.

Signs reading *"Juden Verboten"* became ubiquitous. Jews were verboten in restaurants, parks, schools, theaters. Street lamps and park posts were stuck with bulletins announcing "Boycott Day against the Jews" and new, anti-Semitic laws. Often, obscene graffiti was drawn beneath the bulletins — also anti-Jew.

David predicted a great pogrom. But hyperbole had always been David's style. Sarah listened calmly to his rantings and scrutinized his Jewish features. He really was a fanatic, she thought. If all Jews behaved like this, it was no wonder the Germans were beginning to hate them.

Still, she was affected by David's ideas. Despite all her efforts to understand the new anti-Semitism and how it fit in with the Third Reich, many of the new changes in Germany were terrifying — not so much the progression of the bulletins as the subtle, day-to-day changes in her neighbors' faces. Their eyes could be ice. David's hyperboles scared her when she thought of icy eyes. Even at church, the members seemed to look at her askance. Gertrude, who had always been so friendly, seemed now to be merely tolerating her out of duty.

On March 7, 1936, the Germans invaded Rhineland. The territory was quickly annexed to the Nazi kingdom.

Sarah wanted to celebrate Germany's triumph but found her enthusiasm mixed with confusion and fear.

She quit going to church in July 1936—a month before the Olympics were held in Germany and all the *"Juden Verboten"* signs taken down. Temporarily.

Letters from Hans were coming less and less often. Initially, she had received letters from him weekly, then monthly, and by the time of the Olympics only occasionally — one every three or four months. She told herself that with all the preparations for the Olympics, Germany's postal system was swamped and no one was getting letters. Yet she couldn't help but wonder if Gertrude had told Hans some terrible lie about her. Or had he found someone else in France—someone more worthy of him? An Aryan? She continued to write at least monthly, but her letters were short. What could she say? How could she describe what was happening around her? How could she defend herself to him? Did he even care anymore?

In 1937, Hitler announced the existence of the great German Luftwaffe. In the same year, Hans finished school in France, came home, and joined the army. He was quickly commissioned an officer. Sarah did not even see him; German army officers did not consort with Jewesses.

On March 12, 1938, Austria was annexed to Hitler's domain. Hans participated in the *Anschluss*.

On March 15, German troops moved into Prague, Czechoslovakia. Fanfare and trumpets of victory sounded in the streets of Hamburg. Sarah was moved to tears by the processions but could not tell just what it was that made her weep.

With the new victories came more anti-Semitic laws. On March 28, public statues were withdrawn from Jewish religious communities. Jewish communal bodies were put under the control of Hitler's regime.

On April 26, all Jews were ordered to assess and report the value of their property.

On November 9, a seventeen-year-old Jew named Herschel Grynszpan shot and killed a German diplomat named Ernst Vom Rath. With shouts of "Heil Hitler," Germans, led by the SA, avenged themselves the loss of their representative by beating, murdering, and maiming Jews. Jewish shops were looted, windows smashed, synagogues burned. It was called *Kristallnacht,* the night of the broken glass.

In 1939, all foreign Jews were deported. German Jews were ordered to wear yellow stars. They were forbidden the use of public transport systems. They could receive no Social Security or any government assistance. Synagogues were closed.

On September 1, Germany invaded Poland. On October 5, all Jewish passports were voided. On November 9, a year after *Kristallnacht*, thousands of Jews were rounded up and "resettled." David Sinasohn did not return from work. Nobody had any information about him. Apparently, he had just disappeared.

Sarah wore the yellow star. It was not a religious but a family emblem to her — a coat of arms, as it were. The star did not make her less a Mormon, she felt, though it would not have made much difference to her if it had. Her allegiances were changing as Germany was changing. Her best friend was now her sister-in-law, Zippi. She did not think of Hans anymore, or of Gertrude. And she was certain they did not think of her.

At the time of David's disappearance, Zippi was seven months pregnant with their third child. They already had two sons, Jacob, age five, and Samuel, age three.

Pregnancy made Zippi's face blotchy and swollen, her eyes puffy. Nonetheless, she was regal and the strength of the family. When she brought the news of David's disappearance, she spoke calmly:

"Hello, Mother, Father. I have bad news. Sit, please. Now. David has disappeared."

Aaron, whose bakery had been destroyed a month before, stroked the yellow star on his jacket. He was sitting in the rocking chair. For a long time, he rocked. Slowly, his eyes filled. He said, "My son," and Eva broke into great sobs. Aaron continued rocking, stroking the yellow star.

"He has disappeared before, when trouble surfaced. His politics are suspect, after all. He may be only hiding, waiting it out," Zippi said in her rich, unemotional voice.

Eva dabbed at her eyes with her apron. Aaron continued rocking.

"God will be with him," Zippi said.

Moses, who had been reading in his room, entered and asked, "How long has he been gone?"

"Two days," Zippi said.

"A lot of people are disappearing," Moses said, adjusting his glasses. Moses was sixteen but looked twelve. He was almost as tall as Sarah, though much thinner.

In December, the German army invaded France. David reappeared three days before the conquest was complete. His right cheek was split with a bulging purple scar. Three of his front teeth were missing. He was ragged and emaciated. Indeed, he looked like a derelict. But when he spoke, in a raspy, used-up voice, everyone listened as though he were a prophet.

"He means to destroy us. Hitler. All of us. He wants every single Jew dead."

Hyperbole had always been David's style. But many people believed him now. Including Sarah.


Rabbi Abraham Cohen believed in political detachment. He was not apathetic; he was religious. He believed that any government outside the synagogue, being a human attempt to imitate God's authority, was often evil and usually blasphemous. He concerned himself with his God and with his family, which was, at last, growing.

Deborah had conceived a child so strong it sapped her own strength entirely and drained her cheeks of color. She could bring herself to get out of bed only when absolutely necessary. Her voice was feeble, her gestures weak. But her stomach was firm and big and blossoming. Their child was growing well. With that Abraham concerned himself.

The situation was grave for the Jews in Germany, he knew. He prayed for his fellow Jews who had been ordered to leave their homes or businesses or who had been expelled from the country. But abuse was nothing new for Israel's children. Indeed, their temporary equality throughout Europe had been more unusual than their persecution. The Master had allowed them a taste of prosperity and then reminded them of who they were: the chosen people. The Jews still needed to prove their worthiness. They still needed to be cleansed and refined by fire. But God was with them and would not abandon them. The Master would not forsake his suffering servant. The Bridegroom would not leave the bride. Abraham was certain of it.

Other rabbis were very much involved in politics and intensely concerned about Hitler's Nazism. They persuaded Abraham to attend a conference with them on the morning of January 2, 1940. It was to be held in the cellar of an abandoned apartment building, which had belonged to a prominent member of the synagogue until last month. Abraham kissed his wife good-bye and asked her repeatedly if she was sure she would be all right. She sent him off with the words, "Yes, yes, surely yes."

The reports, given by David Sinasohn and two other young men — good Jewish boys all, Abraham thought, but upstarts — were disturbing, but he could not bring himself to believe what they were saying. Jews being shot en masse. Hitler planning to annihilate the entire Jewish population. Such accusations were simply incredible.

When it was his turn to speak, the good rabbi assured the others that rumors start easily and should be carefully substantiated, or they could terrify whole cities. "Let us keep our eyes on our own plots of land, have faith in God, and trust in Him to protect us."

David Sinasohn stood and looked each rabbi in the eye, one by one, then spoke. "This pharaoh knows not Joseph," he said. "He means to kill us all. Rabbi Cohen, I have seen with my own eyes what he is doing. If you say I can trust what my eyes have seen, then I repeat what I can trust. Hitler wants to eliminate Jews from Europe. It's all in here." He held up a book: *Mein Kampf.* "Written in prison by a madman named Adolf Hitler. He calls us 'vermin.' He wants to eliminate us, Rabbi. He wants that as much as he ever wanted Poland or France or Austria. No, he wants it more."

Abraham breathed in and shrugged apologetically. "That is not the first anti-Semitic book ever written."

"Other anti-Semitic books do not concern me. This one was written by the Führer. He has power, Rabbi, and he is still mad."

Abraham nodded and sighed. "David, I know you would not wantonly lie. I can feel your concern and know it to be from love of your brothers. Still — "

"It's happening now, Rabbi."

"And what do you suggest we do?"

"Defend ourselves," he said. "Or escape."

Rav Hillel stood and quoted the Talmud for nearly thirty minutes, concluding with, "God does not wish us to be defenseless."

Abraham nodded.

The conference took the whole day. Abraham hurried

home, but it was midnight when he arrived. As he approached his house, he knew that something was wrong.

He stopped at his doorstep. There was a strange odor, a strange presence. He looked up at the bedroom window. It was broken.

"She'll freeze," he said, pulling his own coat more closely around his neck as though that could make his wife warmer too.

The odor was stronger inside. A smoky, sweet odor. The living room furniture was disheveled and torn.

"Deborah?" he called, rushing up the stairs to their bedroom. "Deborah?" He flung the door open. "Deborah?"

She was not in her bed.

He flung open the closet door, still calling her. He looked in the bathroom and then called loudly, like a reprimand: "Deborah!" He tore the covers from the bed. Three spots of blood dotted the sheets. Again, louder than before, he called her name. Again, no answer. He ran to Rav Hillel's apartment and cried, "My wife!"

"They were here," said Rav Hillel, embracing him. "They knew we were gone. Someone told them we were gone. This is how they punish us for our meeting. This is how they punish us for our unity. This is Hitler! You see now? Now you believe?"

"They took my wife," Abraham moaned. He cursed the Führer in language he hardly knew he knew and with an inward explosion of hate such as he had never known before.

# CHAPTER 11

On a spring morning in 1940, Aaron called Sarah. "Come sit by me," he said. He was in his rocking chair. She knelt beside him and he stroked her hair. "How old are you?" he asked.

"Twenty-one."

"An old maid." He tried to laugh, but his eyes grew wet, and he bit his lip. "You really should be married by now," he said. "Really, you should be. When your mother was your age, David was already a year old."

She nodded. "Times have changed."

"The world has changed. Human beings have changed. God is asleep somewhere on one of those fluffy clouds, yes?" Again he tried to laugh. Again he bit his lip.

"Maybe so."

"I wanted to talk to you about your future, Sarah. I think,

you know, I think maybe you should take advantage of being a—what is it—a Mormon. Maybe your conversion—maybe it was providential. Maybe God was—"

"I haven't been to the Mormon church in years."

"Still, your name is on their records, isn't this so? Yes?"

"I suppose. Unless—"

"Well, that's good. Don't you see that that is good?"

"No. Why is that good?"

He sighed and rocked. "I want you to talk to one of your friends from that church. One of your Mormon friends. Maybe that boy or his sister. Talk to them. See if they can take you in."

"Take me in! Papa, what are you saying?"

"You are not deaf. Or blind."

"You want me to go away?"

He looked at her tenderly. "I do."

"No," she said, vehemently shaking her head. "I will help here. I want to help here. I want to help Zippi with the new baby. I want to help Moses with his math. I know what you're going to say. I'm terrible at math. I know that. But at least I can try. And Mama—I want to help Mama in the kitchen—"

Aaron's face crumpled around his mouth. He sprawled his hand across his eyes and sobbed.

"Everything will be fine, Papa. I know it will. I want to be with my family. Let me stay."

"No," he cried. "No, Sarah! Oh, my willful, rebellious daughter—no! I want you to go to your Mormons. You decided not to be a Jew. You should not suffer with the Jews."

"I wear the star too," she answered defiantly.

"My little Sarah," he said, softly now, tenderly. "My little rebel. Still so stubborn. And still my responsibility. You will obey me, my little Sarah."

"You're just worried. All the stories, all the rumors. But things will get better. I know they will. They have to! I don't need to go away. And besides—"

"I want you to obey me, Sarah."

"Besides, you know that under Hitler's law, I am a full Jew. Conversion means nothing to him! What good would it do—"

"There are times in life when we simply must trust in the charity of our fellow human beings. If these Mormons were good enough for you to join them in the first place, they will care for you, protect you. Hide you, yes? Isn't this so? If they were good then, they will be good now. It is dangerous for you to be with us. Sarah, I don't want you to be a Jew now."

"I am a Jew! Papa, I know how you feel. I get worried too. But let me stay! I couldn't bear to wonder if something—bad—had happened here. I couldn't bear to be away from you and Mama and Moses and Zippi and the babies. This is my home. You are my family. Of course I am a Jew! Papa, I would go crazy away from you! And you know, Hitler doesn't like crazy people much either." She urged him to smile. He did not oblige her.

"Of course things will get better," Aaron said. "Of course they will. And when they do, we will be reunited and all of this will be a bad memory. Very bad. But for now, you are go."

She tried to joke with him, tease him about being a worry-wart. He was relentless.

"Papa," she said, "I used to have dreams of getting lost in caves. And the worst part was never being lost; it was being alone. Don't you understand? In my dreams I would call to you or Mama, because I knew if one of you were with me, everything would be all right. Always the worst part was being alone. Please, please, Papa, let me stay. Let me be with my family. Please!"

Aaron solemnly shook his head. Sarah knew he would not give in.

"When do you want me to go?" she asked.

"Now. Tonight. At least to see if one of your good Mormons will take you in. Your mother and I have already spoken about it. We agree that it is wise. Best we can do right now . . . "

"I'll go to the Grubbes, then," she said.

"The family of the blond boy?"

"Yes. But he's in the army."

"Fine. You go there, to his home. I will take you now, and we will make this request together."


That evening before curfew Sarah and Aaron went to the Grubbe home. Frau Grubbe, looking very nervous, listened skeptically to Aaron's argument that Sarah's baptism made her a non-Jew.

"But the law says differently," she answered.

"Sometimes a law is wrong," Aaron argued. "Is that not so?"

"There are—problems—for people who help Jews. You know that. Myself, I have no prejudices, but if one is reported to the Gestapo—there are problems."

"If it were necessary, she could be invisible, Frau Grubbe. Yes? You understand me? She could hide in your cellar until this madness ends. Please listen to me. I am not appealing to you as a Mormon but as a human being. As a human being, I ask you to think of your own children. Think what you would do with them if things changed for you the way they have changed for us. Think of your love for them and know that these are the feelings I have for my little Sarah. Twenty-one years old is not little, of course, but to me—please, Frau Grubbe. I promise you we can be discreet. Even in coming here we took back roads and avoided anyone's eyes but yours."

Frau Grubbe gazed at Sarah. "You have grown lovely," she said. "Of course, we haven't seen you for a long time, but I understand that things have been hard of late. I made your baptismal gown, do you remember that?"

"Yes."

"You looked like an angel in it."

"She is an angel," put in Aaron earnestly. "She is an angel, has always been one, and God will surely bless you if you care for her. Your own scriptures—"

"Yes. Yes, I understand."

"I beg you, Frau Grubbe, from the depth of my soul . . . "

"You will come, Sarah," said Frau Grubbe, almost whispering, "when no one sees you. You will never tell anyone where you are staying. You will go out of doors only when it is absolutely necessary."

"Yes," she said.

"Then it is agreed," said Aaron.

Frau Grubbe nodded and closed the door.

Sarah and Aaron hurried home. Sarah gathered a few essential belongings, kissed her parents, her brothers, her sister-in-law, and her nephews good-bye.

She would never see them again.


Gerti proved to be a sullen roommate. She asked why Sarah had not been to church in so long, and why she had waited till now to "take advantage" of her conversion. Sarah answered that her father had directed everything.

"He certainly looks Jewish," Gerti said.

"So do I," Sarah answered.

"Yes, you do," said Gerti. "That makes it dangerous for all of us."

On Gerti's dresser was a picture of Hans, looking very solemn in his uniform. Sarah never asked about him, and Gerti never volunteered any information. For several months, Sarah was a distant and cool houseguest. She felt like the family black cat.

One day, many months after her move, Sarah learned that her family had been resettled. Gerti told her, adding a perfunctory, "I'm sorry."

Sarah was not surprised about the resettlement, and she was not sad. At least they would be together in the east, and after the war they would all be reunited.

She never went outside the Grubbe house. Shortly after her family was resettled, the Grubbes moved her with great secrecy to a cottage a few miles outside Hamburg. It was well hidden by overgrowth. The Grubbes had used it as a summer home years ago, but it was in very bad repair now.

There was a well just outside the cottage, but no food except what the Grubbes brought her. The food came once a week and was delivered with such discretion that Sarah sometimes did not see the deliverer. For long stretches of time, she saw no one at all, though she heard things. She heard shrill sirens, the early warning of an air raid. Full alarm followed, and the cottage vibrated with the hum of planes and the distant drumming of antiaircraft guns. Sometimes at night she could see green bombs like fireworks falling, falling, followed by shrieking black bombs. The barrage of noise rolled in, grew louder and louder, rattled, banged, pummeled the air. The sky seemed haunted with hoarse, groaning ghosts, dragging their chains through the clouds and pounding on all the doors of the world. She could see many fires in the distance; sometimes she could smell smoke.

In May 1943, the bombs were very close. These were fierce thunderstorms, the wrath of God and America. The fires were near, the smoky odors thick. There was a glowing, red haze over all of Hamburg.

No one brought her food during the next month. She had no choice but to leave her refuge and find nourishment. And so she walked into the Holocaust.

# CHAPTER 12

The full-scale murder of the Jewish nation in Germany's ever-expanding kingdom had begun in 1941. The euphemistic Nazis called the murder "the Final Solution to the Jewish Question" and commissioned about three thousand men and officers — called *Eisatzgruppen* — to carry out the mass killing. Everywhere Germany invaded, the *Eisatzgruppen* followed, inciting anti-Semitic groups to riot against the Jews, photographing "voluntary" pogroms, and eventually organizing genocide. Before the death camps were set up, the *Eisatzkommandos* carried out their orders by stripping the Jews naked, forcing them to dig trenches, and then lining them up and machine-gunning them en masse. By the end of 1941 a death camp at Chelmno began functioning, followed shortly by Auschwitz, Belzec, Sobibor, Majdenek, and Treblinka.

In Germany, Jews were told they were to be "resettled for

work in the east" and were systematically transported to their deaths. None was exempted. The first to be killed were the old, the infirm, and the children. The strong men and women had more chance of survival. They could be put to work burning the dead or building roads.

By the end of 1945, the Final Solution had permanently resolved six million "Jewish questions."

Zippi and her three children were resettled in late 1941. They were shot to death.

Moses Sinasohn was torn apart by a pack of dogs when he tried to escape the Nazis during the Sinasohns' resettlement in 1942.

David was worked to death in Buchenwald.

Aaron and Eva Sinasohn were sent to Poland by train. Josef Mengele, the white-gloved butcher of Auschwitz, directed both of them to the line from which none returned. Aaron and Eva were told they were to be deloused. They were stripped, taken to a room marked "Showers," packed in it with dozens of other Jews, and gassed.

Deborah Cohen delivered a baby boy. Both died of exposure in early 1940 enroute to their resettlement.

Abraham's property was seized by the Nazis in June 1941. Two months later, he was told he was to be resettled in the East and was instructed to go to a certain place in Hamburg where he would be conveyed to a train. He contemplated the order. Perhaps, he thought, he would be reunited with Deborah in this unspecified destination. Perhaps she was there even now, waiting for him, with the baby he had never seen (who would now be nearly two years old). Yet something within him said, "Run!"

But of course he would go where the Nazis told him to go. He was a rabbi, the spiritual head of his community. Many of those who looked to him for guidance had also been ordered to report to the train for resettlement. He would have to be with them, to help them, pray with them, strengthen them. To run would mean abandoning them.

Yet there was a new energy filling him, pulling him away from Hamburg, a voice that said, "A dead man cannot lead his people."

He denied the voice again and again, reminding himself of his duty and of the possibility that the train would take him to Deborah.

To leave would be an act of disloyalty, a deed unworthy of one who had been ordained as he had.

He told himself such things all during the night, until the dawn of his resettlement was nearly upon him. When he opened the door of the apartment where he was staying, he whispered to himself that leaving would be a faithless act.

And still came the voice: "The train goes to death."

When he looked outside, he saw an indigo sky. Dawn was barely pinkening the horizon.

He knew then, all at once, that he would run, that he had to run. He had to seek the truth of what was happening around him and had to seek it alone, governed by his own will, not the Nazis. He would trust God, not that crowded train, to take him to Deborah.

He started walking calmly away. When no one could see him, he began to run.

For hours he ran or walked, until nightfall. The next day he did the same, and the next. Abraham made his way through forests and valleys, sleeping during the day, walking at night. He did not know where he was going, could only pray to God for direction. Within a week, he met a group of partisans, young Jews who were working to sabotage the Nazis. They told him about the death camps. Incredulity warped his brow. He still could not fathom that such a thing could be. The Nazis were evil yes, and sadistic, but such a thing — genocide, the partisans were saying — could not happen in a civilized country like Germany.

One of the partisans, a skinny girl with soulful eyes and olive skin, said, "Come with me, if you do not believe."

Together they walked miles, and then she pointed to three hooded trucks rumbling slowly forward on a distant dirt road. "Watch," she said, and the trucks stopped. Nazi soldiers got out. Then more than fifty people — men, women, and children — emerged from the trucks, their hands clasped behind their necks.

"These are Jews," whispered the partisan. "This is a Nazi dumping ground."

Abraham watched the Nazis force the Jews to dig a trench beside the dirt road and then to strip and line up like wooden ducks. Gunshots sounded. Abraham gasped and fell to his knees. More gunshots. Hot tears spilled down his cheeks and neck. Again the shots, echoing through the forest.

Abraham raised his arms to the sky and looked into a bright cloud. "Great Master of the Universe, You must not let this happen," he whispered. "Your people! You must not let this happen! Master of all good! Burn the Nazi idols as you burned the idols of Baal! Show your power! Send lightning, Master of the Universe — lightning to their bloody hands and hearts! Strike the devils down!" Tears rolled down his cheeks and dripped from his jaws to his neck. The Nazi guns reported again.

"You see?" said the partisan.

He sobbed. David Sinasohn and the other "upstarts" had been right. He, Abraham, had been blind. And now it was too late. "Make me like Sampson," he breathed, and he cursed the Nazis again and again and again.

The young partisan repeated what she had already told him about the death camps. He did not question the truth of what she was saying. Not now.

"You are a rabbi?" she asked.

"Yes." His crying, his despair, this nightmare had exhausted him. He could hardly speak. His answer came as a shadow-word: weak, stunned, confounded, bloated with emotion.

"Don't be a rabbi now. They catch you and they make you administer the deaths. In some places, the rabbis sit on councils. It is they who make up the lists of Jews to be killed. Don't be a rabbi now. Shave your beard. Be a warrior."

"Rabbis are making death lists? Rabbis are doing that?" He opened his palms to the heavens, as if his hands were asking WHY? He left them there, as though they could catch God's answer.

"They must, or they die themselves."

"The King of Heaven is letting the rabbis desecrate their ordination?" His fingers strained against this impossible information, curled like claws.

"God is letting all of the Jews be slaughtered. God is dead, Rabbi. God is dead," said the girl bitterly, and turned back towards the other partisans.

Abraham let his arms fall. He began to follow her but then stopped and straightened himself to his most dignified posture. "Not dead," he called. "You will see. He will not be mocked. Not dead!"

She glanced back at him, though she did not wait. "Then he has fallen from Heaven and gotten amnesia. He has forgotten His people," she answered.

"The God who led us from Egypt, who spoke on Sinai—"

"Has gotten very old."

"Do not say these things," Rabbi Cohen said, following her but returning his eyes momentarily to the "Nazi dumping ground."

"Shave your beard, Rabbi," she said, waiting now until he caught up with her. "You look conspicuous."

When they reached camp, Abraham asked for a knife and shaved. He had not seen his bare chin since his eighteenth year. It looked very white to him now when the young atheist gave him a mirror.

For two years, Abraham went with the partisans, fought with them, killed with them. He rarely spoke of God. When he did, the young woman glared.

He thought of Deborah often. He told the atheist about her once and how she had disappeared, how he had tried — with no success — to find her, the rumors he had traced, the stories he had been told. He was certain she was still alive and that they would be reunited soon. But for now, Deborah was simply gone.

"It was a warning to you," the girl said.

"She is alive somewhere and thinking of me, too," said Abraham.

"Perhaps."

"Understand me, when I think of Deborah, I cannot forget God. Job did not forget God, even when his wife was taken from him. I cannot forget God. Deborah would not forget. She still prays on the Sabbath, I am certain."

"My brother was shot," said the girl. "I saw him. They put him up against a wall and did it. I didn't know people had so much blood. It kept coming. He looked at me before his eyes turned glassy. Looked right at me. But it was no prayer in his eyes. It was revenge. That's what he gave to me. That's my mission. For him, for my parents. No prayers for me. I will fight until I die, and God help the man who gets on his knees in my way!"

Three weeks later, the atheist was gunned down as she stole bread from a Polish bake shop. Two months after that, the rest of the partisans, including Abraham, were captured as they prepared to sleep in an apparently abandoned barn.

Abraham was sent to Auschwitz. Josef Mengele directed him to a line made up of young men. They would all be manual laborers. It would be their duty to disentangle the corpses in the gas chambers and cremate them.

The camp was a seemingly deliberate attempt to create and enact the modern, Christian concept of Hell, complete with emaciated, half-naked, tortured men, putrid smells, fire, and endless smoke. In this world, Abraham's job seemed natural. And Abraham, stripped not only of his clothes but more and more of his emotions, fulfilled it as the script dictated: as though he were a machine. He would survive; he swore it. Death would make his life yet another charred testimony against Hitler. There were enough charred testimonies. Abraham would not oblige the Nazis with his death. He hated them too much for that. So he worked as one damned.

He could barely remember Deborah's face. He grew more and more sure that she was dead. (How could such goodness as hers survive in this world?) He was often too tired and too hungry to think of her. Or even to think of God. For months, he did not pray.

Just when it was seeming he had been born in Hell and

had labored in its putridity forever, a new prisoner was assigned to work with him. This new one was young and strong, and he spoke as he worked. Not to Abraham; to the corpses. And to God. The words Abraham knew well: the prayer for the dead. The Kaddish.

"*Yish kadal . . .*"

Abraham stopped and listened. Then, lifting the naked body of a child, he repeated the prayer himself. His voice came weak and unsure at first and then seemed to become empowered by the words themselves as though strength were in their very sounds.

Before he slept that night, he spoke to the young man.

"What is your name?" he asked. One rarely asked names here. The damned were nameless.

"Saul."

"Saul. What you did — how you consecrated the — our job — how you did that — that was heroic."

Saul shook his head. "No heroism," he said. "Just decency. Human decency. My father was a rabbi."

"So was mine," breathed Abraham. "And my grandfather, too."

"I was going to be a rabbi," said Saul.

"So was I."

"But no more?"

"I am not good enough anymore to be a rabbi," Abraham said. "I have read the words of our faith. The Torah, the Talmud, Mishnah, Gemara. I have learned what the ancient rabbis thought and felt. But I am only learning now what Abraham Cohen — my name — thinks and feels when he is away from the synagogue."

"Your name is Cohen?"

"Yes. Cohen."

"But no rabbi?"

Abraham shook his head. "In my youth, I knew the good without knowing the evil. Now I know evil so intimately! I cannot imagine being cleansed of it—ever. I have been desecrated. I have not kept the commandments. I have become what the Nazis wanted me to become: a subhuman creature obsessed with hunger. A body without a spirit. But I will keep this body alive. You, on the other hand, Saul—you are too good to survive."

"Why do you say that?"

"You are not worthy of Hell. You are worthy of a better world. The Nazis will send you there."

"God will protect me," said the young man.

Abraham laughed out loud.

It took less than a week. Saul was shot down for no apparent reason. But even after Saul's death, Abraham continued repeating Kaddish over his dead brothers and sisters. And, as he had sworn he would, he survived.


By some miracle Sarah, too, managed to evade the Nazis for a time. She ate grass and bark and snails and anything she could find to keep her alive. In February 1945, she was discovered and sent to Bergen Belsen. She was put to work cleaning latrines and bunkers.

On May 9, the war ended. Sarah and her fellow inmates were liberated. She weighed eighty-three pounds.

She was caught between two nightmares—her life before her capture and her life after.

The Red Cross transported her back to Hamburg. As she already knew, the city had been mercilessly bombed. Houses she had known were now piles of rubble. The old Catholic cathedral was two Doric pillars and a tilted cross atop a hill of rocks. The familiar Lutheran church had fared somewhat better; its walls still stood, though they were cracked. The building where the Mormons had met was simply gone. All the synagogues, of course, had been razed.

For hours, she walked the ruined streets of her city, not quite ready to approach the place where her own home had once stood. A fine dust floated above the torn-up streets, and a rotting smell permeated everything, as though the air itself were decayed.

Well, Hamburg had paid for Hitler. Germany had paid. But the thought was no comfort, because she was a German and had been a child in Hamburg. Germany had paid for Hitler with Sarah's jewels. Her home, her people, her family had been bartered for a lesson in demagoguery. Power corrupts and absolute power corrupts absolutely. She could smell the corruption, though the odors were not as powerful as those she had known in the camps. Hitler was dead now. Perhaps it was his solitary, absolutely corrupt body that was putrefying the air.

All the houses of her street were gone.

Then she saw her house. Standing.

"How?" she breathed. "How did you survive?"

# CHAPTER 13

When representatives of the Red Cross entered Auschwitz and announced that the war was over and the prisoners free, Abraham stared at them bitterly, thinking them to be disguised SS who had simply untwisted and bloodied their swastikas.

The gates of Auschwitz were opened like the portals of Hell. Abraham was sure that as soon as the prisoners crossed from the world of slavery to the world of freedom, machine guns would sound and raucous Nazi laughter would fill the camp: "Stupid Jews!"

The prisoners looked tentatively at each other, at the Red Cross workers, at the open gates. Finally, one rose and took an unsure step towards the outside world. He looked over his shoulder, shrugged in the laconic way common to all the prisoners, and walked. No machine guns sounded; no laughter. Another stood, and then another. Finally, Abraham stood.

Strangely, his legs felt weaker than ever they had in the camp. He had no bodies to carry but his own, and, emaciated though it was, it seemed heavier than any of the corpses.

Outside the gates was simply open space. Barren trees. Withered shrubs. An occasional weed. The space outside had a different smell from that of the camp—it was strange to him. More strange than lovely. He sniffed suspiciously, looked at his fellow prisoners, shrugged, and turned again toward the camp.

The one who had first ventured to the gates now spoke. His lip curling around his rotting teeth, he lisped, "So, we're free." It was an unemotional statement, without meaning. These men, their heads shaved, their bodies skeletal, their eyes hollow, faces sallow and gaunt, seemed innately prisoners for whom freedom could have no meaning.

Still, a few nodded and tried to smile, echoed the word, "Free."

Abraham looked around himself. Red Cross workers were standing awkwardly nearby. They had brought food, medicine, humanity.

"We should pray," Abraham said, half to himself. The only prayer he had said in the last year was Kaddish. He was not sure he remembered any prayer but the Kaddish.

Another prayer . . .

"*Sh'ma Yisroel* . . . " Hear, Israel. Hear . . .

It was silent outside the prison. Only the breeze moved through the trees and made the dry leaves rustle.

"*Sh'ma Yisroel* . . . "

"*Yish kadal* . . . " The prayer for the dead.

"Let's go back," said one of them. They turned and, slowly, entered Auschwitz again.

The Red Cross provided transport for them the next day,

first to a "displaced persons" camp and later, for those who requested it, to specific cities. Abraham returned to Hamburg and found it wasted. He could not recognize the streets.

He had learned already of Deborah's death. He assumed most of his friends were dead too. Perhaps all of them. Had he not carried the bodies of thousands of his friends from the gas chambers?

He began walking, without direction, simply to see the wrath of God. Then someone called him.

"Rabbi Cohen?"

He turned towards the voice and blinked. A skinny, sallow woman repeated, "Rabbi Cohen?"

He stiffened at the title, squinting at the one who had spoken it. "Sarah?"

"Yes."

"Hello."

"Where were you, Rabbi?"

"Auschwitz."

"Did you see my parents? My brothers?"

"No."

"I'm sure they are dead."

"Yes, they are dead. Where were you, Sarah?"

"Bergen Belsen."

"Ah."

They began, then, walking together.


The survivors slept everywhere: on streets, on the rubble where their houses had once stood, even in trees. Red Cross trucks or other emissaries from charitable nations sometimes brought food and other essential supplies.

Abraham and Sarah stayed in the Sinasohn house with

seventeen other former prisoners. It was amazing, the rabbi told Sarah, that the house had stood. All there spoke Yiddish. Abraham made a vow that he would never again speak the language of the Nazis.

He did not plan to stay long in Hamburg. He was going to emigrate to America, where he had a cousin. He was waiting to receive correspondence and money from him. Both arrived near the end of 1945.

He showed Sarah the letter from his cousin, Simon, and told her he would be leaving within the month, as soon as passage on a ship was available.

"America," she breathed. "You should be very happy there."

He gave his laconic shrug and answered, "Who knows?"

"You will be a rabbi there? A principal in a girls' school, perhaps?"

He shook his head. "I don't think the Almighty would have me now," he said. "I don't know what I will do."

"I'm certain you will find something very good and very profitable, Rabbi Cohen."

He had asked her not to call him "Rabbi Cohen," but she paid no attention. That was all of him she knew, and he was aware she took solace from it. He was the one remnant of her past that had not vaporized. He and the house.

"You—what will you do, Sarah?" he asked.

"Whatever I need to do."

"You would not like to come to America?"

"I have no relatives there. No money. Besides, a poor Jewish woman like me, a refugee who speaks only Yiddish—what would I do in America?"

"Whatever you needed to do, I suppose."

"What are you suggesting, Rabbi Cohen? That I stow away on your ship?"

"You could go as my wife," he said. The thought had occurred to him only vaguely before. He surprised himself by actually suggesting it, and he quickly added, "It would be nothing conjugal, of course. You understand. Only to get you to America. For your protection. I have no desire to have a wife now, no inclinations that way. But I think it would be a good thing. The best thing, given the circumstances. Your reputation would be protected, and we could annul the contract there, on the other side, after you were safe. It seems good to me, since here you have no one. And I . . . You still regard me as your principal, as Rabbi Cohen. So, if I am your principal, then you are my responsibility. Perhaps I have never been released from caring for you."

"Go as your wife?"

"In name only. Do you understand?"

"Yes."

"Do you want to come with me to America, under these conditions?"

"Yes."

A magistrate married them the next day. Three months later, after much paperwork, they boarded the *Lady Liberty* for America.

Abraham knew that in the Jewish neighborhoods of the new land lived Jews who had not even tasted the war, who did not know the word *Auschwitz*. These Americans, many of whose great sacrifice had been to buy coupons for the war effort, could not possibly understand the Holocaust. He was glad they could not. He hoped they would never fully understand it. Of course, some had lost husbands and sons in the war. But not entire families. Not all of their friends. Abraham and his apparent wife would be strangers in a strange and promised land. It would be good to be at home where pain was a foreigner.

Sarah looked much healthier at sea than she had in Hamburg. She was still too thin and sallow skinned, but her cheeks were filling out and becoming pink. And he, his gray-streaked hair and beard back to their former length, looked almost the part of a rabbi.

The trip lasted several weeks, and Sarah was sick many times. Abraham held her as she retched, and then he carried her back to her bunk to wait until she slept. He himself occasionally felt dizzy from the ship's constant, sometimes violent rocking, but he never vomited.

When they saw the lady for whom their ship was named—the Statue of Liberty—Abraham pointed, and Sarah beamed. "And so," he said, "America."

"America," she repeated.

Manhattan rose from the water like a magical island. A new Atlantis. Its rectangular buildings seemed to grow from the sea itself. Gulls circled the ship and cawed at the passengers. When the ship docked, the refugees moved in one united mass for the portals of freedom, and there were processed as immigrants to America. Beyond the processing area was a large hall where a crowd of people waited. A corpulent, bearded man with thick glasses and a felt hat was near the front holding a placard that read "Rabbi Abraham Cohen von Hamburg." Abraham directed Sarah to his cousin, and they pushed through the crowds.

"Hello, Simon," said the refugee.

Simon let his placard fall. His eyes filled, but he did not move. "Abraham," he said.

"Hello, Simon," Abraham repeated, and awkwardly raised his hands.

Simon threw his arms around him and kissed his cheek, sobbing. Abraham, his arms resting on his cousin's back, glanced at Sarah, and waited silently for Simon to calm himself. That did not happen for several moments. At last Simon released him and said, "Welcome." Abraham noticed that American Yiddish sounded different from the Yiddish he was used to.

"I suppose it would be redundant to say that you have grown since our last meeting," Abraham said.

"At our last meeting, I was twenty years old."

"Yes. You have grown."

"I'm still growing." He laughed and wiped his eyes. "My wife wishes I would stop. I keep ripping my seams." He patted his stomach.

"And I have shrunk," said Abraham.

Simon's face tightened. "You are awfully thin," he said, very softly, and began to weep again. "I know you have suffered."

Abraham did not reply. When Simon had his emotions under control, Abraham presented Sarah. "A former student of mine. Now, in a way, my wife. Legally, you understand. Not in a synagogue. I am her protector, nothing more. My former student."

"Sarah," said the American, presenting his hand and bringing his feet together in a stiff sort of a bow, "Shalom aleichem." He kissed her cheek lightly.

"Aleichem shalom," she murmured.

"And now, welcome to America. Welcome home!"

"Thank you," said Abraham and Sarah simultaneously and followed their benefactor to the train station.


It was clear that the war had only grazed the United States. The women in the station wore nylon stockings, lipstick, linen suits with shoulder pads, high-heeled shoes. The men wore pressed suits. The smells of the station were perfume and popcorn.

They boarded a shiny diesel train for Detroit.

# CHAPTER 14

For the first week of their stay in Detroit, Simon and his equally corpulent wife, Ruthie, put them up. Abraham and Sarah slept in the beds once occupied by their hosts' twin sons, now both grown and raising families of their own.

Every day during that week, Abraham and Sarah arose, ate, and went to look for jobs.

Simon had offered to put Abraham in contact with a rabbi, to see about setting him up with a small congregation — perhaps a congregation of refugees — but Abraham had refused, explaining that he wanted an "ordinary" job for now.

"Not as a rabbi?" Simon had asked.

"Not yet."

"Abraham, you are all right?"

"Yes."

"You haven't—you haven't broken with the faith?"

He hesitated. "No."

"But no rabbi?"

"No."

"Why, Abraham?"

"Simon, don't ask. Don't ask. You would not—could not— understand my answer."

Shrugging, Simon said, "As you wish."


Sarah had never worked. The war had interrupted her education, and she doubted she was qualified for anything, though she dreamed of finding a job as a writer or an artist. America, after all, was the land of promise. But there were no ads for writers. Even had there been, she would certainly not have qualified—unless it had been for a small Yiddish news- paper. She knew exactly three phrases in English: "Good morn- ing," "Thank you," and "My name is Sarah."

So, she needed a job that required no English language skills and relatively little education. Seamstress, laundress, jan- itor, maid. There were three possibilities advertised in the paper, all in dress shops. Simon encouraged her to check into the car factories as well.

Big, brawling Detroit with its gleaming, fly-eyed cars was a magnificent maze. She walked down the streets feigning self- assurance, wearing one of Ruthie's old silk dresses, which was much too large. The sunlight hurt her eyes; she had to squint to read signs soliciting help.

She entered a dress shop first, clutching the note Simon had prepared for her: "My name is Mrs. Sarah Cohen. I am a Jewish refugee from Germany. I speak no English, but I can sew and cook and clean very well and I am a quick learner. Your help is appreciated."

A gray-haired gentleman sat at the counter. He accepted the note, read it, then shook his head sadly.

Awkwardly, Sarah backed out.

She ventured next into a diner with a sign in its front window soliciting help. She presented her note to a gaudily made-up waitress, who read and returned it abruptly, saying, "No. I'm sorry."

"Thank you," Sarah managed, and walked towards a little factory, where dresses and shirts were mass produced. It smelled of dye and fabric, and stung her eyes. A young receptionist with dark, wavy hair watched her enter and lifted her brows in distinct question marks.

"My name is Sarah," she said, and presented her note.

The receptionist smiled, nodded, and addressed her in Yiddish. "You sew?"

Sarah let out a startled, delighted gasp and answered, "Yes."

"Good. One of our girls just got pregnant and quit. You take her place, yes?"

"Yes."

The pay would not be much—fifty cents an hour—but it would be sufficient.

Sarah beamed. She had her job. She had gotten it without help or charity. And it hadn't even been hard. America! Where Jews could offer jobs to other Jews—in Yiddish!

Abraham congratulated her that evening when she reported her success. He had not fared so well. He did not elaborate. He rarely spoke to Sarah save to give instructions or ask for food. She spoke to him only to acknowledge the same. But the next day, he found a job in a kosher deli. Then they moved into a dingy apartment a few miles north of Simon and Ruthie, in a city called Highland Park. Both were close to their jobs. Sarah could easily walk to the factory.

Abraham suggested that it might be a good idea for her to secure an annulment of their marriage now, live with a family, and find a young husband who could provide for her the way she deserved.

"No," she answered. "I do not want to be alone yet. I'm not ready."

So they continued to live separately, together.

Sarah usually walked to work when the sun was just above some of the tallest skyscrapers of downtown Detroit. She left the factory at noon to eat lunch, returned to work at one o'clock, and sewed seam after seam after seam after seam until six. By the time she got home, the sun was setting.

It was a hard job, but she was happy with it and with her new life. She loved to walk past the store windows where lanky mannequins modeled the latest fashions — mostly dark suits with thick shoulder pads. One shop sold bridal dresses: rich satin gowns with six-foot trains, full skirted, sequined lace, and dainty net veils. The window display changed every other month. Sarah could stare at the brides for long stretches of time.

Somehow she had gotten herself married but had never been a bride. Indeed, she was not really a wife. Yet when she looked at the brides, she thought of Rabbi Cohen. And sometimes her thoughts were surprising. Sometimes she imagined him holding her, kissing her, being who he was: her husband. Abraham. Sometimes she trembled when she saw the stiff brides and thought of Abraham.

For months, they ate breakfast together, went to work, ate supper together, living as brother and sister, sleeping in separate rooms.

Then one night, Abraham moaned loudly in his sleep. Sarah heard and went to him. She found him sweating, groaning as if he were being beaten and without strength to scream. His mouth gaped open, and his face seemed to slide into it. Still asleep, he was screaming without making a sound. Sarah understood his torment. She wanted to wake him, and she opened her mouth to call him from the nightmare. But only a cry came from her, and it grew to a wail.

Abraham awakened at once and quickly oriented himself. He sat squinting at her. "Sarah," he said hoarsely, so much like the principal who had once scolded her, "why are you crying?"

"For you," she choked.

"For me? Have I offended you? Hurt you?"

"No. I'm crying for you because you won't cry for yourself." Her sobs broke loose. "Oh Lord, God of Heaven," she cried, "how could they? How could you let them? Did you not see? Did you not remember? See us! Remember us!" She wept hard, and Abraham watched her as if from a great distance. "Abraham," she groaned.

"Go back to your room, Sarah. Go back to sleep," he said gently. "Morning comes quickly."

She quieted her sobs and obeyed. She awoke several hours later with swollen eyes and a dull, heavy ache in her temples. "What a sight," she murmured, looking in the mirror above the bathroom sink. "You think they'll let me come to work looking like this?" she said as she gave Abraham his coffee at breakfast.

"You look fine." But he didn't look at her.

# CHAPTER 15

braham found, after a few months of working at the deli, that the smell of fresh, bleeding meat made him nauseated. Still, he could not afford to quit the job. And he was not ready to return to being a rabbi. He did not go to shul.

Once he stepped inside a synagogue and listened to the cantor singing the glories of God. Abraham knew the scriptures and the rhythm of the Hebrew songs. He could have done the singing himself—and better than the cantor. But the cantor seemed to mean every word he sang. His body swayed in pious undulations, as though moved by the breath of God. Abraham could not have sung with such fervor. The words and the Hebrew rhythms were haunting, and he stayed for a long time in the doorway. It seemed to him that if he were to look into the women's section, he would see Deborah.

A young man with glasses and a sparse beard beckoned him to come in and sit. Abraham shook his head and stepped back outside. He was not ready.

Autumn was thick in the air that day. Dry leaves circled the trunks of maple trees. Abraham watched the leaves for a moment and then pulled his coat over his ears and walked to the apartment. He nodded to Sarah as he entered the room and sat on the couch. He was still cold. She brought him coffee, which he drank slowly, and chattered to him in broken English, showing off the new words she had learned that day. She told him about her supervisor, Mimi, a Reform Jew. "She wants us to come with her to shul," Sarah said.

Abraham was tired. "No," he sighed. "Not yet. Not just yet."

Mimi nagged Sarah at work. Sarah repeated the request to Abraham frequently over the next several weeks. "What can it hurt," she said, "our going with her—just once?"

A month later, Abraham acquiesced. He and Sarah joined Mimi for the service.


Mimi was religious by her own standards but only occasionally went to shul. She was infatuated with the rabbi and removed her thick glasses before entering the synagogue. She was quite pretty when her eyes were not shrunken by the lenses. She was also quite blind. Sarah held her arm as they made their way past the worshippers. Mimi stared blankly at Rabbi Silverstein, who was a widower and the father of three small daughters. She whispered to Sarah during a prayer, "He is sexy." Abraham frowned.

"He seems to me to be a very nice man," acknowledged Sarah in Yiddish after the meeting.

Abraham grunted.

"He reminds me, actually, of someone I knew in Hamburg," Sarah said. "A good man. So pious. So good. So dedicated."

"So sexy," put in Mimi.

Abraham glared. "He is a rabbi," he said.

Sarah stiffened, but Mimi was unaffected and went on: "He is a MAN. A widower. And I'm a divorcee. So, who's to say? Really? Who's to say?" She laughed. Abraham's mouth tightened to a white pucker.

When Sarah suggested later that they invite Mimi and Rabbi Silverstein for Abraham's birthday dinner, which, despite Abraham's protests, she had planned for the following Wednesday, he said he did not think it a good idea. Somehow, nonetheless, Sarah got him to agree to it. He was certain the party would be a great impropriety but assured Sarah he would be a cordial host regardless.

When Wednesday came, he smiled at each guest at the door, thanked them for coming, and welcomed them humbly to his home. Ruthie and Simon were there also.

He noticed young Rabbi Silverstein's excruciating shyness around Mimi and wanted to take him aside and apologize. He felt awkward himself, celebrating his birthday in a rented apartment, beside a wife he had never known, in a foreign land, with bare acquaintances. He forced a smile between bites of the meal Sarah had overprepared. After dessert, he waited to see what the topic of conversation would be, or if Rabbi Silverstein would now feel comfortable leaving. Nothing happened.

"It's humid out," he began, and Sarah cut him off.

"No, Abraham. No small talk now. It's time for gifts."

"Gifts?" The word stunned him.

"Of course." She shrugged. "For your birthday."

"Gifts?" he repeated.

Sarah held out a small box wrapped in silver paper. He looked at her eager, nervous face and at the expectant eyes of his guests and took it. The tape seemed too tight. He struggled with it and tore the silver paper. "Oh, I'm sorry," he began, but Sarah urged, "Open, open."

He took the box from the mess he had made and lifted its lid. A gold watch glistened inside it.

"You bought this?" he whispered.

"Yes."

"For me?"

"Yes."

"The money—"

"I saved."

His cheeks grew warm.

"It's beautiful," burst out Mimi.

"Yes, it's beautiful," echoed Abraham uncertainly. "Thank you very much."

"*Mazel tov*," said Rabbi Silverstein.

"*Mazel tov*," echoed the guests.

"Thank you. Thank you," said Abraham, his head bowed, the watch held loosely in his hand. "Very kind."

Mimi sang some popular songs then, urged on by Ruthie and Sarah, and Abraham thanked her mechanically after each rendition.

He still held the watch as though it were a small animal in danger of being crushed.


After the guests left, Sarah approached him. "You are upset that I spent the money on the watch. You are angry with me."

"No. The watch is beautiful. You—why?"

"I wanted to." She looked away.

"Thank you. Thank you very much."

"You're welcome."

He swallowed several times before speaking. "Not long before she was taken," he said, "Deborah gave me a watch."

Sarah closed her eyes. "Oh. I'm sorry."

"No, Sarah, please don't apologize. This watch is beautiful. Thank you. I look at it and—after Deborah gave me the watch, time seemed to stop. Maybe this is a sign. Could it be? Maybe the Almighty—maybe the Master of the Universe moved you to buy me a watch to remind me, to remind me—yes—that time is moving on. Again. Life—"

"Yes." Sarah looked at him and then away. "I think," she said in a lighter voice, "that Mimi is very taken with the rabbi, and he with her."

"She with him, certainly. She makes it obvious. But he? He is flattered, I'm sure. But he has just lost his wife. He needs time."

"Of course," Sarah said. "A man needs time after he loses his wife." She looked at him again. "Of course."

Six months later, Mimi married a sailor and quit her job. Sarah was promoted to replace her and given a good raise.

When she told Abraham the news, he simply nodded and said, "It sounds like a fine opportunity."

"I'd like to buy us some nice things," she said. "Or I'd like to buy you a better watch than that one. A solid gold one—24-karat gold."

When Abraham spoke, his voice was emotional. "I don't need another watch. I like this one fine. But thank you." He reached out to pat her head. She looked at his hand, thought how rarely he had touched her during the three years of their "marriage." He began to move his hand away, but she took hold of it. "Abraham," she said, and made herself look into his eyes. Gentle eyes.

"Yes, Sarah?"

"Abraham—"

He looked away, and she repeated his name three times. She could feel him tremble.

"Please," she said. "You are my husband. Please, my husband. I want you to hold me."

"Sarah—"

She closed her eyes. "Please, my husband."

Unsurely, Abraham brought his arms around her. Then he exhaled a great sigh and wept. She kissed his tears and stroked the back of his head. His chest heaved and trembled against hers. Then gently, tenderly, he kissed her mouth. She held him tighter and cried with him, murmuring, "I love you. I have loved you for so long, Abraham. So long."

He lifted her in his arms, cradled her for a moment, kissed her cheek, and took her to his bed.


The next day they went to Rabbi Silverstein's synagogue and asked to be married in a Jewish ceremony. Abraham shook the rabbi's hand and said, "I, too, am a rabbi."

"I know. We've been waiting for you. Your cousin, Simon, he's a good friend of mine. He prays daily for you."

The next sabbath, Rabbi Abraham and Mrs. Cohen went to an orthodox synagogue with Simon and Ruthie.

Two months later, Sarah conceived a child.

# PART TWO

ISAAC, 1951

# CHAPTER 16

Abraham sat numbly in the hospital waiting room, eyes to the floor. When he heard his name, he stood and watched the tall, Jewish doctor approach.

"Rabbi Cohen?" the doctor said.

"Yes?"

"A son." The doctor extended his hand. Abraham stared at it, stunned for the moment beyond mortal customs. Then he vigorously shook it, repeating, "A son. A son." He fell into his chair. "A son." He was vaguely aware that the doctor was leaving, and he lifted his hand to wave. But he could not see the doctor, for his eyes had filled with tears. And suddenly, the words of the scriptures came to him, filled him, seemed to consume his soul. "Is anything impossible for the Lord?" "I know that my redeemer lives and that He shall stand at the latter day . . . and though worms destroy this body, yet in my flesh shall I see God!"

*"Sh'ma Yisroel, Adonai elohenu, Adonai echad."* Hear, O
Israel, the Lord is our God: the Lord is one.

"In Abraham and in his seed shall all the nations of the
earth be blessed."

Almost imperceptibly, his body began to sway back and
forth in the rhythm of worship.

Simon and an acquaintance of Rabbi Silverstein assisted
with the child's circumcision. The wine was slipped into the
eight-day-old infant's mouth, and the rite of Brith Milah was
performed: the child was put under the covenant of his fathers
and circumcised as a token of his identity. For had not God
said, "My covenant shall be in your flesh for an everlasting
covenant"?

The child, whom Abraham symbolically named Isaac, cried
vigorously as the ritual was performed. Abraham took him in
his arms and whispered, *"Shah, shah,"* and the cries quieted
to whispers. "Oh, this will be a good boy," Abraham prophesied
to all present — and to the world.

Shortly after, Abraham resumed his full rabbinical life.
Rabbi Silverstein taught him about Reform Judaism, but Abraham found the revised traditions too relaxed for his liking,
sometimes almost blasphemous. He eventually headed a small
congregation of orthodox refugees.

Politically he was active, liberal, and unashamedly opposed
to any group that threatened the freedom of another group.
Even from the pulpit he spoke out on such topics as the Ku
Klux Klan and government corruption. He was often quoted
by local newspapers and gained some notoriety.

Sarah supported his views, but kept herself well behind
the scenes. She was content being his wife and Isaac's mother

and with building a good, Jewish home. And Judaism lived in the Cohen household. Even before Isaac could talk, Abraham sat him on his knee and explained the holy days. Isaac's first word was "*Akiba*," though he pronounced it "*Kiba*." He gave this, the title of a venerated rabbi, to his favorite toy: a stuffed bear. During the Chanukah celebration of Isaac's fourth year, Abraham heard him describing the tradition to Kiba the bear.

"Judas Cabas," said Isaac, "lit the menorah, and that's why we get presents."

"Judas Maccabeus," Abraham corrected him. "Do you want me to tell you the story again?"

"I know it already," said Isaac.

"Of course you do. But sometimes it's nice to have a grown-up tell you."

"All right," he acquiesced, as though he were doing a great favor for his father.

"Do you and Kiba want to sit on my lap?"

"All right." He marched to Abraham's chair.

"Now then," said Abraham, hoisting the boy and the bear, "Judas lived when many wicked men wanted to destroy the Jews."

"And Judas was a Jew, yes?" said Isaac, eyes wide, blond-brown hair glistening in the candlelight of the menorah—fully lit, now, for this was the last night of the celebration.

"He was."

"Like us?"

"Like us."

"But there aren't any wicked men today, are there, Papa."

"From your mouth to God's ear."

"Go on. About the war."

"Well, Judas led his fellow Jews in a war, and the wicked men were driven from the land."

"Then he lit the menorah, didn't he, and that is why we get presents."

"Not just yet. There's more. You remember about the temple?"

Isaac hit his forehead and groaned, "Oh, of course."

"Yes. The wicked men had captured the temple, hadn't they? And during the Maccabean wars, well, the Jews recaptured it."

"Hooray for us." He lifted both his arms.

"Amen. But you remember there was very little oil in the lamps of the Temple."

"I remember."

"And the lamps had to burn when the temple was re-dedicated, yes? But the Maker of All is good, so when Judas Maccabeus dedicated the Temple and lit the lamps, the oil lasted for eight days. And so we remember this miracle with candles in the menorah."

"I know," said Isaac, yawning.

Abraham began to sing. "Oh Chanukah, oh Chanukah . . . "

Isaac joined in.

"The festival of lights!"

Abraham gazed at the lit menorah and then at the sky. The candles were lit there, too, he thought, and there were no clouds to cover the glittering lights. He could only weep.

"Papa, why are you crying?" asked Isaac.

"*Shah*, Isaac," said Abraham. "*Shah*. It's only joy."

"Oh," murmured the boy, closing his eyes.


Abraham and Sarah set out a rocking horse and a ball for Isaac after he was in bed, and Abraham mentioned the stars to her. "You should write a poem about the starry night and Chanukah," he suggested.

"I wrote a poem today," she said.

"Yes? Well, let's hear."

"You ready? It's short. And it's in English."

"English?"

In fact, Sarah was very good at English, though Yiddish was still the language of their home.

"All right," she said self-consciously. "This is it:

> They buried me alive and trampled my grave,
> Yet I broke through the tomb
> And lo! Now I bloom!"

Abraham waited. "That's all?"

"I said it was short."

"I like it." He sat on his chair. She knelt beside him, her arm across his knee, her head against his thigh. "Yes, I think it is very good," he said. "Very hopeful."

"Thank you."

" 'Now I bloom.' Yes, that is right. We are blooming, Sarah. Together we are blooming. Through Isaac. Can you see us grow in him? I see my mother in his eyes, and your little brother Moses, and I see myself and you, growing, blooming. It doesn't matter that this part of me is aging." He touched the wrinkles of his face. "It doesn't matter." He stroked her hair. "And these little strings of silver in your hair don't matter either," he said.

"I suppose not."

"So. You have more poems for me?"

"No," she answered quickly.

"All right," he said, but thought, strangely, that she was keeping something from him.

She was. The lines she had quoted to him were only part of a much larger poem, but a poem whose images were so Christian she dared not share it all with her husband.

# CHAPTER 17

Sarah and Abraham had never discussed her conversion to Mormonism. She was not sure he even remembered that she had done it. She herself had only thought about it intermittently over the years. But lately, her dreams had been filled with benevolent, Christian images. A kind-eyed shepherd who said, "Come back to the fold." An etherealized baptism with rainbows and doves. Joseph of Egypt, saying, "Brothers." The dreams were delicious, but when she awoke she would be sweating. She thought she should insist on going through the rites of Jewish conversion and interpreted her dreams as reminders of her interrupted faith. But she found she could not talk to Abraham about either the dreams or her interpretations.

Once, when she saw a pair of Mormon missionaries in their white shirts and ties, a cold nausea spread through her stomach. She watched them chain their bicycles to a lamp post and prayed, "Please, don't let them come here." As though they could know who she was — the way the SS men had. "Please no," she said. "Please no." She went at once to a shopping center and stayed there all morning.

She didn't talk to Abraham about that, either.

Years passed, and the dreams came more and more frequently. By the time Isaac was ten — three years from becoming Bar Mitzvah — she was having them weekly and was troubled by strange thoughts every time she prepared *challah* bread for the Sabbath or cleaned house for a festival.

She often thought about the ritual baths of Jewish conversion, how they cleansed one of all other religions. But what would people think, she wondered. A rabbi's wife . . . She could not talk about it.

Then one day, two weeks before Pesach — Isaac's tenth — while shopping at a large department store, Sarah came across a directory with a familiar name listed as "General Counsel." The name: Hans Grubbe.

As far as she knew, the Grubbes had all perished in the war. It had not occurred to her that Hans could have survived. Yet his name, white letters on the black board, seemed almost to reach out at her and prick her cheeks. She told herself it could not be the same Hans. "Not MY Hans."

She left the department store at once — almost running away — but could not get the name or the possibility of his nearness out of her mind. She sat down on a low cement wall around a fountain. Suddenly she no longer felt like a middle-aged woman but like a seventeen-year-old girl.

She could almost remember what it had been like to love

Hans. Certainly, it had been innocent and naive — pathetically naive — and full of mystery and longing. It was entirely different from her love for Abraham, which included the depth of their shared experiences, their day-to-day trivialities and tribulations, their victories and failures. With Hans, she had discovered love. With Abraham, she had relearned it and felt it flower.

"It cannot be my Hans," she repeated, and told herself she should go to the office just to prove the phantom's nonexistence. "I should go, get it out of my head, finish my errands." But she did not move. "Hans," she said aloud.

It had been so beautiful to love him. There had been a little pain in it, but no agony, no tearing down walls, no bleeding.

She arose abruptly and returned to the department store directory, read his name again, reminding herself, assuring herself, that it was not the same Hans.

Suite 304.

She swallowed, straightened her shoulders, and walked to the elevator.


The door of the suite was open. A slender black girl looked up from the letter she was typing. "May I help you?"

Sarah twisted the strap of her purse and decided to ask where the rest room was and leave. But just as she was ready to speak, the secretary's phone rang.

"Excuse me," said the girl.

Sarah nodded, glancing about her.

Then, just to the right of the secretary, a door opened. A heavy woman exited, saying, "Thank you, Mr. Grubbe."

Sarah stared past the woman. A tall man, slightly bald, with silver sideburns and light, gray-streaked hair filled the door frame. His azure eyes were focused on her. She covered her mouth with her hand. The man squinted.

"Now," said the secretary, hanging up, "may I help you, ma'am?"

Sarah spoke loudly. "My name is Sarah Sinasohn Cohen. I would like to speak with —" She could see him approaching her. Her cheeks burned. She could smell his cologne. Scent of fresh-cut wood. Very right for her Hans. " — with Mr. Hans Grubbe."

"Hello, Sarah. Please, come into my office." He turned to the secretary and said, "Thank you, Lee. Hold my calls, will you?"

Hans's office was lush with plants. He closed the door. Sarah, not looking at him, sat in the large, cushioned chair across from his desk.

"Hello," she said, and was suddenly filled with the images of her past, with the pain of all the years since she had last seen her Hans. Despite her efforts to restrain the sudden, unexpected emotions, she began to weep.

She was aware of a box of tissues being held under her chin. She took one, wiped her cheeks, tried to stop crying. Her stomach ached. "Forgive me." There was no answer, and she raised her eyes. Hans's face was in his hands. She could see his tears curving around his fingers. She took another tissue and passed the box across the desk. "Look at the two of us," she said, trying to laugh. "Almost as silly as we used to be!"

Hans answered with a strained chuckle, his head bobbing rhythmically. He wiped his hands and cheeks and eyes.

"I would have known you anywhere," she said. She spoke in English. She wanted the conversation to be in English. Abraham had made an oath to never again speak German. She respected him enough to keep her tongue free of it as well.

Hans's English was accented but very good. "Not much hair anymore," he said, touching his head. He was not terribly bald, really—he still had a fluff of hair on his crown and temples. His hairline resembled the cap of a barn owl. He was still very handsome. "Cohen, you said your name was now."

"I married Abraham Cohen. Rabbi Abraham Cohen. He was once the principal of my school."

Hans's eyes circled the room as though tracing the memory. "The principal . . ." he repeated.

"Yes."

"HIM? You told me about him. Imagine that—I remember that you told me about him. Wasn't he a gruff old bear?"

"He was a prisoner at Auschwitz. Not many 'gruff old bears' came out of that experience still gruff."

Hans nodded. "Not many of us came out of any of the war 'gruff' as you say. I want you to know, Sarah—I want you to know—" His voice was on the verge of breaking. He cracked the emotion himself with a smile. "Let's go have lunch somewhere. Have you eaten? We have a lifetime to catch up on."

"Several lifetimes."

"Come on, then, let's go. There's a great little deli down the corner. Best pastrami sandwiches in the world."

Abraham would regard her eating lunch with another man as a great impropriety, of course. But Sarah was not so conservative.

"Sounds good," she said.

Sarah ordered coffee with her pastrami sandwich. Hans ordered milk and looked at her significantly. "I don't smoke or drink," she said, smiling.

"Good. The surgeon general—well, you know. But you're

not—you've left the Church, I take it. Of course you have. You're married to a rabbi. Not many rabbis have Mormon wives."

"As far as I know, my name has never been removed from the records—unless all Jewish names were removed from all records when the Führer made it illegal to be a Jew."

The milk and coffee came.

"Actually, I don't like coffee that much," Sarah said, testing it. "I could give it up if I wanted to. But I haven't answered your question, have I? Well then, I go to the synagogue; we celebrate the Jewish festivals. That makes me a Jew."

"You sound uncertain," he laughed.

"Maybe so. How about that? A rabbi's wife who wonders if she might be a Christian. When I joined the Mormon church, I did it largely for you, of course. But, you know, there was something in me that wanted it. Something in me that loved Mormonism. I felt sensations—lovely sensations, you know— as a Mormon. I can't remember now what they were like, only that I felt them. Maybe it was misguided love."

"Maybe."

"Or a need to have all the answers to all the universal questions supplied. I don't know. I don't know what it was. But I did feel something. Of course, during the war, my identity was defined for me. Brutally defined."

"Yes."

"I was a Jewess—convert or not. It seemed natural, after the war, to continue in that identity. And I don't need to mention that I stopped having any lovely feelings while I was at Bergen Belsen."

"You were there? They sent you there?"

"Yes."

"They found you?"

"Yes."

"But my family—Gerti—no one turned you in?"

"Your family was very loyal to me."

"They were killed, you know," Hans said unemotionally. "Bomb strike."

"Yes. I heard the bombs. I thought they must have died."

"Died. Yes."

"Anyway," Sarah continued, sipping her coffee, "there were no lovely feelings at Belsen, except in memory. And I didn't like to remember much after a while. So, you asked me if I have left the Mormon church. The answer, of course, by your definitions, is that I have. Of course I have. But you know, I still remember things sometimes that touched me deeply back then. Sometimes they touch me now too."

The sandwiches came. Sarah commented that they looked very good and bit into hers. "You, I assume," she said, "are a fine Mormon. Certainly you are. Probably a bishop by now. Did you ever go on your mission?"

"No. And I'm not a bishop."

"When did you emigrate?"

"A decade ago. Germany is—there are so many memories there. So much. So little. I had no idea you survived. I assumed you were killed in the raids. Or—"

"The world is full of little surprises, yes?"

"I didn't help your cause much," Hans said.

"Your family saved my life."

"My mother was a very good woman. A very good woman. Gerti told her not to help you. Gerti told her your presence might endanger our family. I got many letters from my sister begging me to persuade Mama to turn you in. Discreet letters, of course. The censors—well, that's not relevant here. What is relevant is that I did nothing—either for you or against you. I think you should know that."

Sarah dabbed at her mouth with her napkin. "I suppose you felt you needed to tell me that, Hans. It doesn't shatter me. I knew Gerti felt threatened by me. With good cause. My presence did endanger your family."

"I did need to tell you. And I need to tell you that I'm so grateful you survived. And that I'm so sorry—listen to me! As though one German citizen could apologize to one Jew and erase the Holocaust!" He chuckled weakly, then grew quiet. "How impotent we are, Sarah," he whispered.

She did not answer. She sipped her coffee and finished her sandwich. She said in a soft, melancholy voice, "I remember so vividly what you looked like as a young man that first Sunday I saw you in the Mormon church. Your hair so blond it shimmered. You were like a vision. You know, the Führer must have seen someone very much like you when he decided to create a Master Race of armies of handsome, blond, blue-eyed men. Like you."

Hans sighed. "Please, Sarah—"

"There was a guard at the camp," she continued, "who looked like you. Very much. He could have been your brother. Sometimes, I would gaze at him and wonder if it could actually be you, distorted by hate. It was not you, was it?"

"No."

"No, of course it wasn't. So, you are not a bishop. You are still a Mormon, though, yes?"

"Now I am. But I lost track of the Church for a time. The circumstances—"

"Hans, you don't have to tell me the circumstances. They don't concern me, do they?"

"I suppose not."

"You are married?" said Sarah.

"Yes. My wife is an American. Norma. From Detroit. She was a Red Cross nurse. I met her in France. We have three beautiful daughters."

"Abraham and I have a son," Sarah said.

"And you are happy, Sarah?"

"Yes," she said. "Yes, I am very happy." She finished her coffee. "Hans, I want you to know I hold nothing against you or Gerti. Your family saved my life. You saved my life."

"My mother is the one who saved you. My mother was — she was a very good woman. A true Christian — excuse me; I should not use those terms with you."

"Well, if my name has not been removed from the records of the Mormon church, then I am a Christian, too," she said, and patted his hand.

She invited Hans to bring his family to her home for supper the Sunday following Passover.

# CHAPTER 18

Sarah cleaned the house for a week in preparation for Passover. The night before the Pesach feast, she hid bread crumbs behind the closet door, on a chair. Then ten-year-old Isaac found and collected the crumbs. In the morning, the crumbs were burnt. Passover began.

On the Seder plate were bitter herbs, recalling the bitterness of slavery; a roasted bone, symbol of the lamb sacrifice; apples, wine, nuts, and cinnamon, representing the mortar the ancient Israelites slaved to make for the Egyptians; parsley dipped in salt water, for the greenness of spring and the tears of the Hebrew slaves; a whole egg, symbol of the newness of life; three pieces of matzoth for the three ancient divisions among the Israelites. A cup was reserved for Elijah, the invited but invisible guest. Abraham's chair was cushioned as a reminder that the Jews were now free to sit or lean as they chose.

Isaac squirmed in his chair, eyes glowing. Abraham nodded to him.

"What makes this night different from all other nights?" the child asked, and Isaac and Abraham spoke the ritual conversation. The family recited the plagues of God on the Egyptians and remembered the passing over of the Angel of Death.


Sarah had already told Abraham of her visit with Hans, but she had not mentioned the dinner invitation she had extended to the Grubbes. This she did after the Passover festivities.

Abraham became silent—a different silence from his frequent, meditative lulls of speech or his pensive brooding. A tense, dark silence. He disapproved her invitation; she could feel it.

"You do not like the idea of having them—having—" she struggled with the word "Mormons—come here?"

"It's not that."

"Hans's mother saved my life. I owe his family an unpayable debt."

"I understand that," he said softly.

"What is it, then?"

He moved uncomfortably in his chair. "It's you."

"Me?"

"And Isaac."

"Isaac?"

"Never mind," he said, waving his hand. "Invite them. Of course, invite them. You are right. You are indebted—"

"I think we need to talk about it."

"Then talk, Sarah," he said, nodding and smiling his familiar principal's smile.

She trembled. "We have never spoken of it."

"No."

"I didn't know if you even remembered."

"I remember. A Jew remembers. A Jew's heritage is to remember."

"My name, as far as I know, is still on the records of the Mormon church."

"Well then, there it is. The issue."

"I—if you want, I will undergo the ritual baths as a new Jewish convert."

"You mean you do not consider yourself a Jew?" His eyes forced hers away.

"My blood is Jewish," she answered.

"And your beliefs?"

"My beliefs," she echoed. "They are—oh Abraham, my Abraham, I don't know. I have thought about it so much. I have been tormented!"

"I don't understand. What, Sarah—what has tormented you?" He spoke slowly, as though he were addressing a child.

"Independence," she blurted. "Don't you see? I have never actually decided who I am, what *I* want—. Or rather, I decided once and had my decision rescinded. Always, someone has told me what I believe, who I am, what I shall be. My parents, Hans. You. I'm behaving like a silly adolescent, I know, but it is not silly. Somewhere—deep, deep inside me—there is still a Christian. A Mormon. She's there with the child who once drew insulting pictures of you in Hamburg. And sometimes, she wakes me up in the middle of the night and speaks to me as though our conversations had only been interrupted by the war and by you and by Isaac." She spoke the last words so rapidly that they merged in a frantic line of sound.

"Of what does she speak to you?" He spoke slowly, kindly. Still the gentle schoolmaster. Gentle as a lamb. But frightened.

"Of—I don't know! Of hope?"

"Hope? In Christianity?"

"Yes."

"Sarah!" It was like a plea from the dead.

"Abraham, before the war, I used to listen to the Bible stories and imagine that they prophesied of the Messiah."

"They do. Of course they do."

"And that the Messiah was Jesus of Nazareth."

"Even after the—what we went through—you can believe that Messiah has come already?"

"In the camp, I tried to tell the SS that I was a Christian. I wanted to feel that I was different from the other prisoners. Less deserving of punishment. Actually, I hadn't attended church for months before I went into hiding. But I pretended, for a while, to be a convert. At the beginning of my captivity, I used to try to remember the Christian stories. I used to try to identify with Jesus, try to remember his crucifixion, his resurrection. But the fantasy didn't last. One day I imagined his disciples going to his tomb, finding the stone rolled away, telling each other he had been resurrected, then discovering the body all bloody and beaten and rotten with death just outside the sepulchre. After that, I didn't think about Jesus any more."

"And now?"

She sat for a long time with head bowed and lips pursed. "I believe in God," she said. "I believe in Him, and that He has saved my life, just as He saved the Israelites from the Egyptian chains. I have been resurrected. And I find I can believe in resurrection."

"You needn't be a Christian to believe in resurrection. Many Jews believe in resurrection. That is not the issue."

"And I find I can believe in the resurrection of Jesus." She closed her eyes.

"And the six million of our brothers and sisters? Have they been resurrected by Jesus?"

"Abraham, I understand so little. Least of all do I understand myself. I have so many questions, so many doubts about everything." Tears rolled down her cheeks. "I am trying so hard to make sense of my life, to understand it. When I think of Messiah, I cannot imagine just a king—someone—an antithesis to Hitler—who rescues his people like Superman or Robin Hood. When I think of Messiah—my Messiah—I think of the Nazarene. I think of him dying without justice, just as those six million of our brothers and sisters died—"

"You compare him to them?"

"Yes! Abraham, it is not in spite of our sufferings that I can believe in such a Messiah; it is because of them. Messiah is the suffering servant, as the Jews are. Why should we say that we must live to be worthy of our suffering if suffering is not for our good? If Messiah is like the refiner's fire, why should he keep us from burning? Or from being burned? Why, Abraham, did Moses take the children of Israel from their slavery in Egypt and lead them to the wilderness? Forty years of wandering in the wilderness! Forty years for the Israelites to die so that their children could fight to possess the promised land! Why? Why did he not just deliver them?"

"Why? Why? Because they disobeyed the law! The Almighty said, 'Thou shalt have no other gods before me.' They worshipped idols. Idols, Sarah! False gods! The gods of their enemies! The gods of those who wanted to destroy them!"

Sarah was silent. "Forgive me," she managed at last.

Abraham did not answer. She continued softly. "We are told, 'In all thy ways, acknowledge Him.' Not 'In all *His* ways.'"

The little girl within me—the little resurrected girl—sometimes she wants to acknowledge God as the Mormons do. But she is a very silly child, of course. I know that. Silly and, sometimes, blasphemous. As an adult, I am a Jew, Abraham. I am. I love our customs, our faith. But that silly little girl is alive inside me somewhere."

Abraham folded his arms. His lips and chin were puckered white. He looked even older than his years.

"I am hurting you," she continued. "I know I am. But— oh Abraham, don't abandon me. Please try to understand. It has hurt me so much to fight that little girl all alone, to remind her of the—the stupidity—of Mormonism when—when she is me. Me! My childhood. My life before the . . . "

Abraham's face relaxed. He nodded slowly. Sarah wondered if he were praying. "I know," he said at last, and she saw that he was talking to her, not God. "I have sensed your wavering."

"If you wish, I will undergo the ritual baths," said Sarah.

"You will have to make that decision. I will not tell you what to do. But, regardless of what you decide, Isaac will be a Jew. You will never tell him of your 'silly childhood.' You will discuss nothing of this with my son."

"Of course," she said, feeling more strongly than she had in years that she was in the principal's office.

Abraham was a polite host to the Grubbe family, though Sarah could sense his nervousness. The dinner conversation revolved around the Michigan weather, the baseball season, and the world economy. The war was not mentioned.

Norma Grubbe was a corpulent, silver-haired woman who looked at least ten years older than Hans. But she laughed so

easily and heartily that Sarah could understand how Hans had
fallen in love with her — she, an American Red Cross nurse; he
a soldier with a shattered ankle and a broken heart.

Their three daughters resembled Hans much more than
they did their mother. All were blue-eyed, blonde beauties.
The prettiest among them was nine-year-old Elsa, with hip-
length, platinum hair, curled at the ends, and enormous, thick-
lashed eyes. Even little Isaac, who claimed to hate all girls, saw
that she was pretty and stole glances at her all during dinner —
glances that were not unnoticed by his father.

Elsa did not seem to be aware of her beauty. Her older
sisters carried themselves with haughty posture and pretended
to be much older than they were. But Elsa was timid and very
like a restless nine-year-old. It was obvious she would much
prefer something more casual than the ruffled pink dress she
was wearing. And there were clearly more important things in
her life than her own good looks: trees to climb, horses to
ride — or dream of, fields to explore. When Isaac invited her
to see his tree house, she eagerly accepted. Abraham suggested
that the other girls might enjoy seeing it as well.

With the children away, the grownups continued talking
in innocuous circles. Abraham mentioned the charitable foun-
dations with which he was working; the Grubbes acted dutifully
impressed.

As the family was leaving, Norma Grubbe invited the Cohens to their home the following Sunday for a "kosher" dinner.
Sarah smiled up at Abraham, who was blinking rapidly as he
said, "Certainly."

Isaac waved to the departing guests with his parents. "That
Elsa is some chick," he said.

"Almost enough to make you stop hating girls, eh?" Sarah
teased.

Abraham repeated the word *chick* as though he were a very old and deaf man. "Chick? Chick? A girl is a girl and must be treated as such. With respect. All girls. Even shiksas. Which, of course, Elsa is."

That night, Sarah's insomnia was fierce. She awakened at two in the morning and became quickly aware that Abraham, too, was awake and that he was crying very softly. She reached across the mattress and took his hand. "What is it?" she asked. He embraced her. She could feel his tears, wet on her forehead.

"What?" she whispered.

"Master of the Universe," he groaned, "there is still so much hate, so much bitterness in me. Oh Master, Creator of all good, cleanse me!"

"Abraham." She stroked his cheek and kissed it.

"Those children," he sobbed, "those beautiful children — they make me remember!"

"Deborah?"

"Deborah. Why should he — that man — one of Hitler's soldiers, have three beautiful daughters, when Deborah and our baby — " he cried.

"Talk to me, Abraham."

He clung to her. "I'm afraid of losing you, of losing my son to the goyim again. I'm afraid!" His whole body shook.

Sarah kissed his cheek. "You will not lose us," she promised. "Shall I call Norma and tell her something has come up and we won't be able to go to their dinner Sunday?"

"No," he sighed, wiping his eyes. "No, of course not. They are good people. If I begin running from every threat now, I may never stop. I need to learn to trust you and to let my son grow." He wiped his cheeks. "No. We will join them. We will learn to be their friends. Abraham will trust in the Lord."

Sarah kissed him again. "I want you to know," she said, "that I am a Jew. I will be with you always, in everything."

Abraham seemed relaxed at the Grubbes' home. He did suspiciously eye the food Norma Grubbe served, and she quickly assured him, "All kosher. A Jewish friend of mine helped me prepare it."

Sarah found that she and Norma had much in common. She felt that Norma could be a real friend and, after they had returned home, asked Abraham's permission to make "permanent friends" with her.

He took a long time to answer. "I will not control your life. They are lovely people. We will learn, certainly, to be their friends."

She knew he was bothered by the prospect, and so she did not call Norma, though she had promised she would. But after a month, Norma called her. Soon they began visiting each other weekly, sharing recipes, knitting sweaters, going shopping. Occasionally, the Grubbes' daughters accompanied their mother.

When Isaac was made Bar Mitzvah, the Grubbe family attended the synagogue. Sarah was content that the two families were on the best of terms and that Abraham was neither bitter nor afraid.

# PART THREE

## ISAAC, 1966

# CHAPTER 19

By the time he was fifteen, Isaac was nearly six feet tall — two inches taller than his father — and had a rich tenor voice. It was obvious, much to his parents' concern, that he liked Elsa, who had grown even prettier and more graceful.

Abraham spoke to his son more than once about the temptations of adolescence and the importance of marrying within the faith. Isaac responded by rolling his eyes and assuring him, "Elsa is a friend, nothing more, nothing less. That won't change. Don't worry. I'll marry a Jew, when the time comes. Right now, I'm too young to get involved with anyone. Elsa included. She is so rotten at geometry, though, that I have to help her. And sometimes she needs advice, so I give it. As a friend only, Papa."

It was true that Elsa needed help with geometry and that she needed advice — particularly in the social sciences: there were six boys interested in her. Two of them had already beaten each other up. She was not yet old enough to date, in her parents' eyes, but that didn't stop the boys from pursuing her.

Isaac found the situation amusing and flattering. While other boys fought over her, Elsa chose to be with him nearly every day. They had developed a custom of meeting in the Birmingham Public Library, which was midway between her high school and his yeshiva, after classes dismissed.

When Elsa turned sixteen and was thus officially old enough to date, Isaac continued assuring his father that she was no more than a friend. But when Abraham suggested the two of them were seeing too much of each other, Isaac broke into a sweat. It occurred to him as though for the first time that the day would actually come when he would not be able to be with her. He would marry a Jew, she would marry a Mormon; and the two of them would raise their families in different parts of the country and never see each other again. This thought actually hurt him in his chest, as though his heart were really breaking.

He spoke to Elsa about it one day as they walked through the park by the library. Elsa would be going to her high school's junior prom with the quarterback the following weekend, and Isaac would escort a frail thing named Anna Goldbaum to a yeshiva party the same night. "You know, someday this will be a permanent arrangement," Isaac said. "You'll marry some Mormon bishop and I'll marry some little Jewish girl, and we'll never see each other again. We'll be like—"

"Like my father and your mother," Elsa said.

"What?"

"You know."

"Know what?"

"Well, they were once, you know, boyfriend and girlfriend. She joined the Church for him and everything."

"What church?"

"The Mormon church, of course."

"Come on, Elsa. That's ridiculous."

"Are you serious? You really don't know about any of this?"

"My mother was never a Mormon," he scoffed.

"Yes she was. Listen, Isaac, this is history. Honest-to-goodness history. Imagine you needing help with history! Golly!"

"Elsa, are you suggesting that my mom and your dad—"

"Before the war."

Isaac leaned against a tree. "Do I understand this correctly? You're saying that my mom became a Mormon?"

"Your parents don't tell you much, do they," Elsa said, taking his hand. "Have they told you about the birds and the bees?"

He made a brief grin and rolled his eyes. Then he said very softly, "Mom never mentioned any of that."

"You mean about the birds and the bees?" Elsa had a habit of sucking in her lips and widening her eyes when she was teasing.

Isaac acknowledged her mischief with a strained laugh.

Elsa moved closer to him. "You have beautiful eyes, you know, Isaac," she said. "They are like a doe's eyes. Especially here, by this tree. Like a doe's eyes peeking out of a thicket." Her lips parted slightly.

They were alone, the park was filled with piney smells, and Elsa was beautiful. Isaac leaned to her. He paused four inches from her lips. "You're not lying to me, are you, Elsa? You've never lied to me."

"No, Isaac." She sucked in her lips again. "You really do

have beautiful eyes." She drew her mouth closer to his. He could smell her spearmint breath and feel its warmth.

"Come on, Elsa," he said, his hand moving to her cheek. "About my mom. That's true?"

"Yes," she breathed, her eyes closed part way.

"Rats, Elsa," he whispered, drawing nearer to her, "why do you have to be so beautiful?" He brushed her lips with his, then kissed her. He had never kissed a girl in his life, let alone a shiksa. And what was worse, Elsa responded fully.

"Isaac, I love you, you know," she said.

He kissed her again and then said, "I love you too. Rats! My father was right. It's going to hurt, Elsa. I know it is, because eventually we're going to have to break up. It's going to hurt like—"

She kissed him before he could finish.


Isaac volunteered to help his mother with the dishes that night—a rare offer. She accepted dubiously, certain he was buttering her up for some monumental favor.

Abraham retired to his study, and Isaac began stacking plates.

For a moment, neither Isaac nor his mother spoke. But Isaac watched her and she smiled self-consciously at him.

"Something you want, Isaac?" she said.

"Yes."

"Go on, then."

"Information."

"Yes?"

"Did Hans Grubbe use to be your boyfriend?"

"Who told you that?" she answered calmly, lowering her eyes to the plate she was washing.

"Elsa."

"You've been seeing a lot of Elsa. Too much, maybe? Don't you agree? You're almost university age, now. Maybe you should start looking seriously at some of the girls in the synagogue."

"I'm taking Anna Goldbaum to the yeshiva party tomorrow, did you forget?"

"That's right. She's a nice girl. Nice girl."

"She looks like she's about twelve. And she has acne."

"Looks, my dear, are not everything."

"Was Hans good-looking when you two were young?"

"Hand me that pot, will you?"

"Mama, you're evading the issue."

"What issue?"

"Is it true that Hans was your boyfriend when you were a girl and that you got baptized a Mormon for him?"

She turned to him as though she had been slapped. "Hans and I were friends. As for Mormon baptisms—Isaac, I am a Jew. I have suffered for being a Jew. My family was killed for being Jews. In my youth, I was capricious. Now, I have put away childish things. I don't even consider the subject relevant anymore. Besides that, it's private."

"Sorry," he said. "I didn't mean to step on any toes."

Suddenly, Abraham's deep voice bellowed from the hall-way. "Isaac!"

Isaac turned, "How long have you been there?"

Now Abraham was gentle. "Long enough. I'd like to have a talk with you, if you don't mind."

Isaac dried his hands on the dishtowel, mumbling, "I'll bet it's not about the weather."

Abraham's study was filled with books of Jewish lore,

Hebrew poetry, scriptures, and commentaries on the scriptures. On his desk were neatly stacked reams of paper and
more books. The walls held pictures of old rabbis, who seemed
to Isaac to know all his secrets and to have their eyes focused
on him. But the worst eyes were his father's.

Abraham sat at the desk and gestured to the armchair. Isaac
sat in it.

For a long time, Abraham just looked at him. He pursed
his lips, breathed deeply, and said at last, "*Nu,* Isaac."

Isaac tried to look innocent. He succeeded only in looking
timid. "Yes?"

"I think maybe you have something you would like to tell
me? Yes?"

"Really?"

"Please go on."

"Elsa?"

"That is the subject, I believe, yes."

"She is still a good friend."

"You kiss your good friends?"

"I kiss you. I kiss Mama."

"You kiss Elsa, too?"

He shrugged. "Only one time."

"You kissed her the same way you kiss Mama and me?"

"Sure," he said, squirming.

"On the cheek?"

"Sure," he said, adding softly, "there too."

"On the mouth maybe, too?"

"Maybe," he said.

"You don't remember?"

"I remember," he said sullenly.

"You think maybe you are involved emotionally?"

He nodded, eyes downcast.

"And she with you?"

Again, he nodded. "I know you warned me," he said.

Abraham was silent. He breathed deeply. "Isaac, there is nothing more painful than losing someone you love. Nothing in the world. It is better, I think you will agree, not to start something that will have to end painfully. She is a shiksa."

"She could convert." He had not thought of this possibility until now.

"Of course she could. Her father had the same idea once with regards to your mother. Of course Elsa could convert to Judaism. You think her parents would take kindly to you if she did that? Or, let us not forget, you could convert to Mormonism. Couldn't you?"

"No," he said firmly. The answer was a reflex.

Abraham picked up a pen and held it horizontally in his hands, stroking it. Isaac noticed how his father's hands shook, as though palsied. "I have always believed," Abraham said kindly, "that each person must live his own life, make his own decisions, that no one has a right to control another person. No one! Neither governments nor churches nor parents. Free will is a sacred gift. I will not take yours away. But as your father, I have an obligation to you, to protect you. Therefore, as your father, I must counsel you to break off whatever it is you have with Elsa. Don't see her again. I will not stop you if you should choose to disobey me. I will, however, as my duty demands, remind you of the law: 'Honor thy father and thy mother, that thy days may be long upon the land which the Lord thy God has given thee.'"

Isaac nodded. "I won't see her again, if that's your wish."

"It will be your choice. I have only complicated things. I have complicated them because now your choice is not just between seeing or not seeing a very pretty girl but between obeying or disobeying the counsel of your father, who loves you more than Elsa could dream of loving you."

"I understand," said Isaac.

"Good." Abraham put down the pen. He stood, walked towards his son, and kissed him on the forehead. "You are a good boy."

The next day, Isaac took another route home and did not even approach the library. That evening, he took Anna Goldbaum to the yeshiva party and had a terrible time.

# CHAPTER 20

Isaac kept his promise — for a time. It was torture. Everything reminded him of Elsa. The sky was her eyes, the clouds her hair. He could pick out Elsa's features on his classmates' faces: her nose on one boy, her mouth on another. Death from a broken heart, he determined, was worse than cancer. After a week, he decided to go to the library one last time — to explain to Elsa what had happened. Only to explain, he told himself, sketching her picture during Hebrew class.

He ran all the way to the rendezvous point after school. But Elsa was not there. He waited for an hour. She did not come. He phoned her from a booth. Norma said Elsa was studying with a friend and not home yet. Isaac had a feeling the friend was male. "Please tell her I phoned," he said.

The next day he went to the library again. Elsa was there this time. With another boy.

Isaac's eyes met hers. She glared. Her lips turned down in a defiant pout. He approached the table where she was sitting with the boy, whom he guessed to be Kevin Goff, the quarterback. "Excuse me," Isaac said. He turned to the boy. "Isaac Cohen," he said, extending his hand. The boy shook it.

"This is Kevin Goff," said Elsa.

"Elsa is sort of my mother's godchild," Isaac said. "I have a message for her, if you don't mind. It'll just take a minute. It is private, though."

Kevin looked skeptical but shrugged.

"Maybe we could go into a conference room, Elsa," Isaac suggested.

The pout on Elsa's lips tightened. She nodded and stood.


"I don't want to talk to you," Elsa whispered as he held the door for her.

"You don't have to talk. Just listen."

"Do I scare you, is that it?"

"I thought you said you didn't want to talk."

"I'm listening."

"My father doesn't want me to see you anymore."

"Who told him you were seeing me?"

"He overheard me talking to my mother."

"And why did you have to tell her? What is this, some kind of subconscious subterfuge?"

"What are those? Words from your vocabulary list? Don't pull them on me. We're way ahead of you in the yeshiva." He sighed. "Sorry. I'm being rude. But you could at least be understanding."

"I don't want to be understanding," she said feebly. "You're going to make me cry."

"Don't. Don't, please. I don't want to hurt you. Elsa, do you know how hard this week has been for me?"

"Not nearly as hard as it's been for me. I figured you had been killed or something. Then one of my friends saw you on a bus. You were just standing me up, that's all. I think you're scared. I think you're scared of me and of feeling anything you can't control with your Jewish logic. I think you're one big coward."

"That's about the size of it," he said. "I shouldn't have expected you to understand."

"Kevin has asked me to go steady."

"Congratulations."

"I guess I'll tell him yes."

"I'm sure you'll be very happy. I hear he makes great passes."

She glared again. "I guess that concludes the talk, doesn't it. Maybe I'll see you around, Cohen." She turned to the door.

"Elsa —"

"Shut up, will you?" She walked to Kevin and kissed him on the cheek. Isaac's own cheeks burned in response. He waited in the conference room, glancing up every few moments to see if Kevin and Elsa were still there. When they left, arm in arm, he was aware of two distinctly focused emotions: anger at his father, and bitterness towards Elsa. He doubled his fist and hit the desk, and then he buried his face in his hands.

He was about to leave the library but was suddenly struck with the thought that once he left it, he would never return. His exit would be permanent. He would never set foot in this library again. He would never again see Elsa.

He wandered around the stacks, perused a few books,

looked in the card catalogue. He looked up "Love," "Pain," and then "Mormon." There were a number of references under that last word, most notably the book he had heard Elsa refer to several times: the Book of Mormon.

He walked to the shelf it was supposed to be on, and immediately saw the title. A black leather book. He took it from its place, glancing quickly around himself. "Written to the Lamanites," he read, "and also to Jew and Gentile." He had assumed the Book of Mormon to be the Christian version of the Talmud—a commentary on the New Testament, perhaps a statement of Mormon doctrine. It seemed, however, to be an independent book of scripture, a translation of an ancient record. "And also to the convincing of the Jew and Gentile that Jesus is the Christ . . . " Ancient, Christian scriptures. He closed the book and was about to put it back on the shelf but found himself thinking of his mother, wondering if she had read it. He scrutinized the cover and carried it to a private desk.

For three hours, he read the Book of Mormon. It was somewhat like the English version of the Torah in style and poetry, but it was clearly a Christian work, complete with visions of the Messiah, who was personified in Jesus of Nazareth. Isaac found it easy to be objective about the book. He felt no need to finish it—he knew its biases after his brief reading session—but he checked it out anyway and hid it in his briefcase. A demon within him wanted his father to discover the book, wanted to punish his father for so suddenly and so righteously taking Elsa away.

The claims of the Book of Mormon seemed farfetched to Isaac's skeptical mind, but it was clear to him that the author or authors had genuinely believed what they had written. There was something in the words they had chosen, the imagery, the emotional pleas, which indicated not that the book was true but that its authors believed it was.

Isaac did not share their view. If the Messiah had come, he had failed miserably to redeem Israel.

It took him only a week to read the book, and he quickly returned it to the library. He found, however, that he could not get it out of his mind. It had been written by converted Jews; of that he was sure. Either by Jews or by some Gentile who was familiar with the Hebrew tradition.

Gradually, in quiet moments between classes or even between scriptures in Hebrew class, he began to be aware of little questions in his mind. He found himself wondering if there were any way the Book of Mormon could be true—if Jesus could have been the Messiah and the redemption of Israel a spiritual, ongoing redemption, as the book claimed.

He cast these thoughts from his mind as soon as they surfaced, but they kept coming back. He studied the Torah furiously. Still the questions and dissident thoughts came.

He was a Jew, he lectured himself. The Torah and its commentaries had been written for him. THEY were his books. Not this Book of Mormon. The Book of Mormon was for Christians, and Christians had abandoned the Law. Christians were a deceived, cultish, sadistic people.

Still, the questions.

He answered defiantly: Jesus of Nazareth had not come in glory. His Messianic claims had ended with his crucifixion.

Yet the words of Isaiah echoed: "He was oppressed, and he was afflicted, yet he opened not his mouth: he is brought as a lamb to the slaughter, and as a sheep before her shearers is dumb, so he openeth not his mouth . . . " The suffering servant.

He thought of the Christian revivalist crusades he had seen on television. "Do you accept Jesus as your personal savior, my son?" "Yes! I believe! I am SAVED!" A little old man on his knees. No faith in himself so he has to find something in which to have faith. Relinquishing his mind and conscience as he exults, "I am SAVED!"

It could not be so simple. Had six million Jews died so that a little old man could shout, "I am SAVED!"?

"My kingdom is not of this world . . . " Jesus had said.

The Book of Mormon accused the Jews of "looking beyond the mark." Was it possible they had looked towards the mountains waiting for the armies and had not seen the hosts of Heaven all around them?

Isaac suddenly wanted everything to be Jewish. He wanted no reminders of that outside, wicked, deceptive, seductive world. He was grateful his father had forbidden him to see Elsa. He understood his father now. His father did not want him to associate with anyone who might jostle his faith. It was love that moved the command. His father had said there was nothing more painful than losing someone you love. But there could be something more painful: wounding someone you love. He would never be able to do it. If (God forbid!) his questions became too overwhelming, if (God forbid!) they caused him to fall from the faith — even convert (God forbid) — he would simply stop questioning.

He became quiet. He attended the synagogue faithfully, hoping each time to find new bonds to Judaism. But the questions did not stop.

One evening, after six months of unrest, he offered to do the dishes with his mother again. She looked at him warily.

As soon as Abraham went to the study, Isaac asked her,

"Did you believe in Mormonism when you converted? Or did you do it just for Hans?"

She inhaled. "Why?"

"I need to know."

"A person can make himself believe anything he wants to," she said.

"So you did believe."

"I suppose. Hand me that plate, will you?"

"Do you believe it anymore?"

"Of course not."

"Did you read the Book of Mormon?"

"Isaac, do we have to talk about this?"

"Does it make you so nervous?"

"Yes!"

"Why? We're devout Jews. Can't we talk about other faiths without getting upset?"

"You bring up memories I do not wish to recall. I am ashamed of the capriciousness of my youth. I am ashamed of my disloyalty."

"I read the Book of Mormon."

Sarah dropped the plate she was holding. It broke in the sink. "You don't have enough to study at the yeshiva?" she asked mechanically, gathering the broken pieces.

"More than enough, believe me."

"Why waste your time on the Book of Mormon?" she said, feeling around in the water for more pieces.

"I don't know."

"I think I got all of the pieces. There now."

"Mama, what if it is true?"

"Isaac, you're being ridiculous."

"And you're being defensive. Why are you so nervous? Do you think it could be true?"

"Why don't you talk to your father about it?"

"Wouldn't it be easier just to stab him?"

"You shouldn't have read that book."

"I didn't say I think it's true. Of course I don't. I just asked if you thought it could be. A person has to be objective. A person has to live his own life."

"That's right. And you live it." She began scrubbing the counter. Isaac noticed that one of her fingers was bleeding. When he pointed it out to her, she cursed. It was the first time he had heard her use such language.


After a few weeks of fighting images from the book—olive trees, iron rods, Jesus Christ as Messiah—Isaac returned to the library and checked out the Book of Mormon again. He read it in two days, setting aside his yeshiva studies.

The authors of the book seemed to speak directly to him, to challenge him, grip his doubts and shake them. He spoke back to their words, argued with them, debated them. As a last gesture of objectivity, he decided to pray about the book as one of its authors, Moroni, exhorted. Then he would put it away, out of his mind and life, having tested it fully and found it a lie.

That night, before retiring to bed, he read the final verses of Moroni, which were mostly quoted from Isaiah. These words he knew. They had been written for him and all the sons of Israel: "And awake, and arise from the dust, O Jerusalem; yea, and put on thy beautiful garments, O daughter of Zion . . ." He thought of Chanukah, the captured Temple retaken, the lamp within it lit, and all the daughters of Zion in Sabbath clothes walking towards it, as though rising from the dust.

"Strengthen thy stakes and enlarge thy borders forever . . ."

He thought of the tents of the Festival of Tabernacles, celebrating the season when the Lord had made all Israel dwell in booths after he delivered them from Egypt.

"That thou mayest no more be confounded . . . " He thought of Passover, the four questions.

"That the covenants of the Eternal Father which he hath made unto thee, O house of Israel, may be fulfilled." He thought of Yom Kippur and the sacrificial lamb.

"Yea, come unto Christ!"

Could it be?

He prayed. "Master of the Universe, God in Heaven — could it be? I will ask you one time. Could it be?"

He thought then of Joseph of Egypt, imagined him standing before a gilded throne, speaking to his brothers — they who knew yet did not know him.

"Brothers!"

And he, Isaac, was there, one of the brothers who had put Joseph away, sold him into captivity.

"Brothers, I am Joseph."

The words were Hebrew.

"Does my father yet live?"

"Yes," said Isaac, kneeling. "He's alive."

"Come near me, my brother. See who I am. Come near me, I pray you."

Isaac obeyed and, as he approached, saw Joseph's form change until he was no longer Joseph but another man, more familiar and more glorious.

"Come and see," said the other, holding out his hands. In them, and in his feet, were wounds.

Isaac gasped. "No! Who did this?"

"These wounds I received," said the other, "in the house of my friends. But be not grieved nor angry. These are tokens of my atonement. God sent me before you to preserve life. Behold, my brother, I have engraven you in my hands and in my feet. You are written here."

"Could it be?" Isaac said, touching the marks. "Could it be?"

"God sent me before you to preserve your life by a great deliverance. Isaac, I am your deliverer."

"Lord!" said Isaac. "It was you?" Sudden certainty washed through him, warm and sweet. As though emanating from his very cells, the words filled his body: "This I have always known."

It all fit.

All through his life, he had sensed that he was imitating someone. Often he even found himself thinking: "It was like this for him too."

For whom? A grandfather, a father. All the sons of the commandment.

But there was one particular, unseen Him.

He wore the yarmulke too. He spoke our words. (*"Sh'ma Yisroel . . . "*) He knew our law. He celebrated our rites. It was like this for Him too.

At times when Isaac spoke the prayers, he could almost hear that other's voice, prompting him not just with the words but with their meaning and feeling, with the pain of the ages, the faith of the faithful.

Behind every ritual, every prayer he had spoken, every covenant he had made, stood this other: the suffering servant, the shepherd, Father, Son, King.

It had always been Him. The Holy One of Israel. "God with us."

It was His blood on the Hebrew doors. His strength that scourged Egypt. His power that sculpted fire into word on stone tables. His light that burned in the Temple. His pain that comprehended their pain.

He was one of us. Lived as one of us. Died as one of us. Was lifted up to heal us. He, the Mighty God, the Anointed One, was redeemed from death as we were redeemed from slavery. He was the deliverer, the one we knew and did not know.

The Lord God restores. Jehovah saves. *Yeshua*.

The words burned in him: The Lord is *our* God! The Lord is *one!*

"You have always known."

"*Sh'ma Yisroel, Adonai elohenu, Adonai echad.*"

It had always been Jesus before him — the One God of his faith. Messiah.

Messiah!


"Good morning, Isaac."

His mother's voice, calling him distantly.

His body was still warm, almost tangibly joyful, as though light were pulsing from his heart.

He would arrange for missionary discussions, he told himself, before noon.

"It's late," called his father.

The joy did not evaporate, but Isaac shrank at the sound of Abraham's voice.

"Oh, no," he breathed. "No, I could never do that to him! Please, Lord, tell him what you've told me! Don't give me such gifts that make me dance on my father's heart!"

And to this thought came a distinct, almost audible answer: "Do you think, my son, that you love Abraham better than I do?"

# CHAPTER 21

Sitting at the breakfast table, Abraham looked weak to Isaac. His lips were curved in their characteristic half-smile. He was reading the newspaper. His hair was slightly disheveled (so white!) but his beard was immaculately groomed. His eyes, behind reading glasses, were bloodshot. It struck Isaac that they seemed to be bursting with suffering.

At the yeshiva, Isaac was pensive. How many times had his father preached that one must do what his conscience tells him, even in the face of contrary masses? One must live one's own life. It was a family theme. Isaac was not frightened of the decision that lay before him, only tormented by it.

During art class, he sketched a scene from the Pharaoh's court, wherein Joseph held out his hands to his brothers. "Brothers, I am Joseph." Joseph was young. His eyes were like Abraham's and Jesus'.

"Very good," said Reb Raubvogel, picking up the sketch before Isaac was aware that he was being observed. "Yes, this is very good indeed. The best you have done yet. Excellent. Excellent."

"It must have been inspired," murmured Isaac, an ironic smile twisting his lips.

He rushed home from school that day. He wanted to speak to his mother before his father arrived. She would be hurt, but she would have to understand. She, too, had once become a Mormon.

He arrived just as Sarah did. She was carrying two large sacks of groceries, which he gallantly lifted from her arms.

"Thank you very much," she said.

"Mama, we have to talk."

She looked at him, probing his eyes, and then backed away. "Everything is all right, no? Your father—"

"Mama, I'm going to break his heart."

She began walking rapidly. He followed, struggling under the weight of the groceries. She held the door for him and whispered as he entered, "Please don't."

Silently, they put the groceries away and then sat at the kitchen table. "*Nu,* Isaac," she said, as though imitating his father.

"A person has to follow his conscience," he said.

Sarah put her forehead in her hands and rubbed her temples. "You love—or think you love—Elsa very much, don't you?"

"I haven't spoken to her in a long time."

"Sometimes, when we are in love, we can imagine a perfect world, a perfect faith, a perfect union, because love, at the onset at least, is perfect. Beautiful. No suffering. And all an illusion."

"You loved Hans like that, and that's why you joined the Mormon church?"

She nodded and said again, "*Nu*, Isaac."

"Elsa is not involved in my decision," he said quietly.

Sarah began to cry. "I love your father so much," she said. "So much more than I ever loved Hans or imagined I could love him! We have not lived an illusion—unless it's been the devil's illusion. But life has been complete with him. He is so good, Isaac. Can't you, just for love of him, for honor of him and his goodness—"

"Can't I what? Be dishonest with myself? Mother, no. I can't. He has trained me too well for that."

Sarah laughed at the irony and then wept loudly. It struck Isaac that there was more behind her weeping than she let on.


Supper was especially quiet that night. Sarah dropped her fork on the floor five times and finally left the table, complaining of a headache. Isaac watched his father and braced himself. He began to speak, but found he could not.

He cleared the table, told his father he would wash the dishes, and watched him go to the study. He filled the sink with scalding water and burned his hand when he immersed the plates. Groaning, he told himself, "Be brave. Brave!"

When he finished and the kitchen was clean, he made his way to Abraham's study, said a silent prayer, and knocked. He was surprised to find his mother there, too. As soon as he saw her, and then his father, he knew she had told him.

Abraham removed his glasses slowly, revealing damp, red-rimmed eyes. Hoarsely, he spoke. "*Nu*, Isaac . . ."

Isaac stood straight. "You have taught me to live my own life, to make my own decisions, to—"

Tears brimmed in his father's eyes. Isaac had seen him cry before, many times, but not like this. This was agony. The sight summoned his own tears. He knelt beside the older man and said, "I love you very much."

"And you would do this—this thing?" Abraham asked, his whole face caving in. A person would look like that after being hit hard in the mouth, thought Isaac.

Abraham turned away as Isaac stood. "I prayed about it, Papa," Isaac said. "I feel—"

"You inherited your feelings from me! But have I not taught you how to think, how to govern your heart with your brain?"

"I have thought," Isaac said quietly. "Thought and thought and thought and thought. Joseph's brothers did not recognize him until he spoke to them in their own language and told them who he was. Don't you think it is possible that we will not recognize the Messiah until he speaks to us in our language and tells us who he is—don't you think it's possible he has been among us already and we have not recognized him?"

Sarah gasped and held her hands to her mouth.

"Have you seen the German girl?" said Abraham.

"Once. To tell her I would not see her again. She is going with another boy."

"And I'm sure you want her back, don't you?"

"It's not Elsa, Papa. Not Elsa. This was my decision. If you want, I will not see Elsa again."

"The shiksa has already taken you from us. Why should you not see her? Live with her? Lie with her?" His cheeks, which had been pale when Isaac entered the study, were crimson now.

"No, Papa," he murmured.

Abraham fell back in his chair. His eyes moved up and down Isaac's body, measuring him. Then they closed.

"Papa!"

"You go," said Abraham slowly. "You go." Tears seeped out his closed lids. His cheeks grew less red; the purple veins in them seemed to stand out, collecting the color.

Isaac left silently and closed the door behind him.

# CHAPTER 22

Abraham rarely spoke over the next few days. He left for long stretches of time. Usually he walked to a park, where he would stroll under the apple blossoms. He spent hours in the synagogue, praying, his body swaying back and forth with such intensity that he seemed at times to be swooning.

On Friday evening, he greeted the Sabbath alone — the first time he had done so since Isaac's Bar Mitzvah. In his study, he read the account of the ancient patriarch for whom he was named, and the sacrifice on Mount Moriah. He plaintively asked God, "You could not have provided a ram in the bushes? He had to be given to the rites of the goyim? For what purpose?" The question echoed in his head and stung his eyes.

All day Sunday, he prayed for his son and for himself.

On Monday, he went walking again, and found himself

before a small shop across the street from the park. On its
door was printed "Ex-Mormons for the Lord." Abraham raised
his brows and walked inside to the tinkling of bells. A gangly
blond boy with acne and an unctuous smile said, "Can I help
you?"

Abraham glanced around. The shop was no bigger than
the walk-in closet in his and Sarah's bedroom. It had probably
been intended for storage. It was packed with books and pamphlets.

"This is a — bookstore?" Abraham asked.

The boy nodded. "We represent ex-Mormons."

"Ex-Mormons?"

"Disillusioned — "

"I can figure it out," he said, fingering a pamphlet. "I
suppose you are one of these 'ex-Mormons.' "

"I am."

"Your parents? They are ex-Mormons too?"

The boy laughed. "Hardly. My dad is a bishop and my mom
teaches Primary. You know what that means? You're Mormon?"

"I'm a Jew," said Abraham.

"Not a Mormon?"

"My son wants to be Mormon."

"Well, send him to me," said the boy.

"Does your father know that you — "

"Of course."

"And how does he react?"

"The way any Mormon bishop would react, I guess. Prays
for my salvation. He's never even bothered to read the material
we have here. It might raise questions. He doesn't like to think."

"And you like to think?"

"You bet."

Abraham smiled halfheartedly. His eye caught a pamphlet with the title: "The Fall of the Book of Abraham." It seemed directed at him. A slap in the face, a fulfillment of some primordial prophecy. "The Fall of the Book of Abraham." There would be no Book of Abraham for Abraham Cohen. Isaac had left the faith.

"All of this, I suppose, made you leave your faith," Abraham said, gesturing vaguely.

"Well, just read it!"

"I don't have the background to understand it. I'm a Jew. It is my son who wants to be Mormon. He wants to leave the faith we have taught him and join this church. Do you know what it does to a parent to have a son—"

"I can imagine," the boy said, then looked away, blushing.

"Can you? And still—. No. Every man must have his free will. No man can usurp free will. No man should try to usurp it. Thank you for your time," he said, touching his hat.

The boy repeated, "Send him to me—really," and shook Abraham's hand, slipping two anti-Mormon pamphlets into it.

Abraham accepted the leaflets, but thought as he did that he would like to meet the boy's father and tell him the heavens were yet moving, balancing the heartaches of earth. Somewhere, an atonement was being wrought. Abraham's son was replacing the other man's son in the Mormon faith, and he, Abraham, was bearing the pain of barrenness. This was the lot of the Jews, was it not? How well he could tell of it!

He walked back through the park, stopping beneath an apple tree to watch bees hover between blossoms.

The bees were borne up in the abeyance, conveying pollen, keeping the natural balance in order, feeding the hive, and quietly dying. He thought how lovely the world is, and how treacherous.


When he got home, he went to Isaac's room, put the anti-Mormon leaflets on his bed, and retired to his study. He said nothing to his son about the ex-Mormon and did not initiate any conversation about the leaflets at supper.

# CHAPTER 23

For a month, Isaac met with the missionaries every Wednesday at the Mormon church. The yeshiva was in its last week of the school year when he followed through on his decision to become a Mormon by setting a baptism date, and by going to the library to find Elsa and tell her.

She was there. With Kevin. He approached the table where they were studying, their heads tilted together. He cleared his throat. Elsa turned her head quickly towards him. Her surprised eyes became soft and sad. "Isaac," she murmured.

"Do you mind, Kevin? My mother wanted me to—I need to speak with Elsa. For just a moment."

Elsa stood. Kevin shrugged and grunted. It occurred to Isaac that he had never heard Kevin speak actual words. "I'll be right back," Elsa said.

Isaac and Elsa walked to the conference room. Isaac opened

the door for her. Their eyes met as she crossed the threshold. "Hello," he said.

"How are you?" Her voice was very low.

"Fine. I'm fine. I've thought about you."

"I know. I've thought about you, too," Elsa said. "I wanted to apologize. The last time we were together—"

"It doesn't matter. What matters is, Elsa, I have news." He stopped talking and laughed. "I sound like a Jewish mother, don't I?" he said, then looked deep into her eyes. "I'm going to join your church."

"Come on, Isaac. Don't joke like that."

"No joke."

"Come on. Your father—"

"It's killing him."

Her eyes widened and quickly narrowed, as though they had swallowed the information. "Isaac, you're serious."

He nodded.

"Not for me. Please, don't do it for me. I could never have that—I love your parents too much to do that to them."

"Not for you. I read the Book of Mormon. I prayed. I'm doing what my father has always taught me to do: following my conscience."

"And killing him in the process."

"Yes. It's hurting him very much."

"Oh, Isaac!"

"I want you to be at my baptism. Saturday at 11:00."

"Saturday. The Jewish Sabbath. Isaac, are you sure about this?"

He turned away. "You don't even sound happy about it."

"Happy? I'm—it's just I didn't expect it. I didn't think— Isaac! You're really telling me the truth?" She stepped towards him. Isaac nodded in Kevin's direction.

"Yeah, I'd better get back to him. He's driving me crazy, Isaac. I'm surprised he doesn't buy me a leash."

Isaac opened the door. Elsa closed it and said, "One thing I have to say. I—you know, I've missed you. I still love you. I'll always love you."

"I love you, too. Now get back to your boyfriend."

Winking, Elsa obeyed him.

Saturday dawned bright and warm. Isaac lay in bed for a long time, listening to his father make preparations to go to the synagogue. A pair of monarch butterflies hovered outside his bedroom window, flirting in circles around each other. He was at peace with himself. Still, he cringed when he heard the front door open and close.

Isaac got out of bed, washed, and went to the kitchen. His mother was there, looking at him mournfully.

"Good morning," he said.

"Are you going to do it?" she asked.

"Yes."

She turned to the stove and touched the *latkes* she was making. "Shalom Shabbat," she murmured.

Hans Grubbe baptized him two hours later, whispering before the ritual, "You can't possibly know how much this means to me."

Since junior high, Isaac's plan had been to work after the yeshiva let out and go to a rabbinical college for his rabbinical degree, his *smicha*. He wanted now to go on a mission.

He asked his father if he should find an apartment. Abraham said simply, "No." So he continued living at home, maintained

activity in the Church, resumed a serious relationship with Elsa
(who had broken up with Kevin a week after Isaac's baptism),
and held a job at a Ford factory, saving most of his money for
his mission. He never discussed his plans with his father and
continued to eat a kosher diet. He turned nineteen on June 7,
1970.

Before he submitted his mission papers, Isaac told his
parents his plans. Both were acquiescent and sad, as he had
expected they would be.

The call arrived on July 17. He got it from the mailbox
before either parent got home. For a moment, he held it in
his hands, then ripped it open. He scanned the first page. It
contained information on international vaccination certificates.
"An international mission," he thought. The second page was
a letter from the Language Training Mission in Provo, Utah.
The next was a letter from the Church Office Building—official
information for all missionaries. A form letter. The third began,
"Dear Elder Cohen . . . " This was not a form letter. He scanned
it quickly. His eyes stopped on the words: Germany Hamburg.

"No—please, not Germany," he said aloud.

Germany. Hamburg, Germany.

Germany.

He would have to learn the language his parents refused
to speak or have spoken in their home.

Germany, Hamburg. How could he tell them?

He called Elsa. "I have to talk to you," he said.

"You got your call? Did you, Isaac?"

"Elsa—"

"It's to Germany, isn't it," she said soberly.

"Hamburg."

"I had a feeling."

"I have to talk to you."

"I'm here. I have all night. Come now, if you can."

He went immediately. Elsa was waiting for him in her front yard. "What did your parents say about it?" she asked as she hugged him.

He kissed her cheek. "I haven't told them."

"Oh boy."

"Amen."

"I heard of a kid once who wrote the General Authorities and requested a change in his mission call. And they gave it to him."

"I could do that. I could. Save some grief. Elsa, I can't tell you how I felt reading those words. Germany. Germany! Hamburg, Germany! My parents have given me some terrible feeling about that place. I just get the darkest feeling about it—as though I were there, hiding or being forced to go to a concentration camp. And now someone is telling me I have to go back."

They went inside. Isaac noticed all the German crystal and Hummel figures, the fine lace curtains, the goblets in the china closet—all artifacts of Germany—as though he had never seen them before. The houses in Hamburg would probably resemble this one, he thought: simple, practical, tasteful, highlighted with exquisite workmanship. His eyes rested for a moment on the lamp shades.

"You don't have to go there if you don't want to," Elsa said. "You can explain it to the Missionary Committee. They'll understand. I'm sure of it."

Isaac sank into the couch, wove his hands behind his head, closed his eyes. Elsa put her arms around him, her ear to his chest. "I can hear your heart beat," she murmured.

"That's a relief. At least the shock didn't kill me." He hugged her. "Quite a coincidence, isn't it."

"Yes."

"The Missionary Committee couldn't possibly have known my background. Yet they call me to Hamburg. To the people who tortured my people, murdered my family."

"It's almost like a judgment."

"Against me?"

"Against them. Or for them. A judgment of mercy."

He whispered, "They don't deserve mercy; they deserve justice!"

"So did the murderers of Jesus, and he forgave them from the cross."

He looked away.

"Maybe your call isn't a coincidence, Isaac."

"I'd rather go to Israel."

"Write the Missionary Committee, then," she said dully.

"You were the one who suggested that."

"Or how about this? Go on your mission to Hamburg, but take a little gun and mete out justice to all the ex-Nazis you can find. While you're at it, you may as well start with my father."

Isaac grimaced. "Look, I'm sorry. It's just that — the language. German! German, Elsa!"

"*Deutsch*. I speak it, you know."

"I know. Try to understand. Please try."

"I want to. I really want to. You know what I think? This call isn't just for you; it's for us. Something way back in our pasts — something we didn't experience personally — has to be set right. It's deep, Isaac. Very deep."

"I'd rather go to Israel."

"Oh come on, you know if you went to Israel you'd join some guerilla outpost."

"Hamburg."

"It's your decision, my dear."

"I have to go, don't I? There's a reason I was called there."

"I think so."

"Hamburg," he repeated. "Hamburg."

Elsa nestled her head in the crook of his neck and took his hand.

"If you get married while I'm being a missionary, Elsa Grubbe, I absolutely will not send you a present," he said.

"I promise you I will not get married while you are being a missionary. I'm much too young. Now, I may get engaged . . . "

He kissed her hard.

CHAPTER 24

He prayed for an hour before approaching his parents with the news. He considered not telling them at all, announcing simply that he was going to be a Mormon missionary for two years, and that they would not hear from him during that time. But he couldn't keep a secret from them.

He asked them to come to the living room. They sat on the sofa by the fireplace and waited. He realized, looking at them, that either or both could die during his mission. His mother: hazel eyes that cried easily; large nose, full lips, rosy, veined cheeks; jowls that were growing more and more flaccid; deep, frowning wrinkles in her forehead that did not fit her personality and which (he was sure) had not been there before his conversion. His father: much older looking than his mother; his wrinkles like road marks on a map; his large, brown eyes — Isaac's eyes — bloodshot and distorted by bifocal glasses; his hair and beard snow white as one would imagine an aging prophet's. He looked so old. But his voice could still fill a canyon. Isaac assumed he himself resembled a slightly taller version of his father minus forty years. But Isaac was growing taller and stronger; Abraham was shrinking and growing weak.

"Mother, Father," he began, reverently, as though addressing royalty. "I know I have made you suffer terribly. If there had been a way I could have followed you without disobeying my conscience, I would have done it. I swear I would have. And if there were any way now—"

"You have news?" interrupted Abraham.

"I am going to be a missionary, Papa. My mission call has come."

"*Nu,* Isaac . . . "

Isaac's eyes teared. He had not expected them to, not so suddenly, and he turned away. When he gained control and looked at his parents, he saw tears under his father's eyes. Abraham, of course, knew. Abraham knew everything. And Sarah, his mother—she knew, too.

"Germany—Hamburg," Isaac managed.

"You have to go?" his mother said, as his father repeated, "Hamburg!"

Isaac wiped his eyes. "I don't have to. It is a choice. And I have made it. I have decided. I—I want to go. I want to know that place, the people there. In a way, my roots are more in Hamburg than in Michigan. I want to go."

"You imagine yourself, perhaps, as a sort of Moses," said Abraham dully, "going back to Egypt just to have a look around, to curse the Pharaoh face to face? You see yourself like this?"

Isaac shook his head. "I won't go with hate."

"You see yourself, maybe, like Moses again, going back to Egypt to apologize for any inconvenience his escapades might have caused? You want to see the place of our captivity, perhaps, and tell our captors that everything is fine now, do you?" The old man's voice was full. Isaac felt the hate in it, understood how malignant it was, understood why he himself had cringed when he had seen the words of his call.

Again, but weakly now, Isaac shook his head. "Can we hate them so completely?" he murmured.

Abraham leveled his index finger at the boy like a gun. All the wrinkles in his face deepened; his eyes bulged. "You think one Israelite mother who watched an Egyptian soldier kill her baby could look at the pyramids without the saliva welling in her mouth? You think one Israelite slave could walk with an Egyptian taskmaster without thinking of murder? You think one Jew who lived through the horror—no, Isaac, you do not understand. You—you can worship the one who is more re-sponsible than any other for our persecution. You may worship him, wear the cross if you want. Of course. Wear the cross upon which the world crucifies the Jews. Surrender your heart, your mind, your will to your Jesus. Pray to him from dawn to dusk. Pray to him in German, if you will—if you have left us so thoroughly. I still had hope . . . "

Isaac turned to his mother. Her face was pale and emo-tionless. "I knew it would be hard on you," he said.

Sarah bowed her head. Abraham echoed, "Hard!"

"I want you to know I believe in what I am doing. I didn't convert to wound you. I believe in my religion."

Slowly, Sarah's eyes filled. Still she did not speak.

"Go then," said Abraham in a very low voice. "See if Ham-burg still smells of—it's so far away."

"Not so far," murmured Isaac.

"Far. Far. It is death. Hamburg is death. You could not possibly know, you could not possibly imagine what they did to us. The desecration, the mutilation, the brutality." His eyes clouded. "Kosher executions for their entertainment. You could not know!"

"You suffered what you did for your faith—the price of your faith," Isaac said.

"I did not suffer of my own volition. I was the victim of THEIR sins. A far better position than a *kapo*. Do you know what a *kapo* is, Isaac?"

"No."

"One of us who joined them to postpone the inevitable. One of us who became one of them. You realize, don't you, how easy it is to bend the ends of a cross?"

Isaac stood, fists clenched, mouth tight. He breathed, "Don't."

"Don't," repeated his father, pleading.

"Don't," said his mother, still staring straight ahead, speaking, apparently, to both men.

"I need time to think," said Isaac, and left the room. He walked fast, praying. Behind him, his father quoted Isaiah:

" 'Cursed be he that turns to Egypt for help!' "


Slowly, Abraham turned to Sarah. "One decision. So easy. So easy and so complex. Your decision. How could you have known?"

"Please," she said.

"The worst of it," he said softly, "is that I'm afraid one of these days you will tell him you believe in his Mormonism, too. You think I don't see you tighten when he makes some fanatical statement? You want to believe it too. It would make life so much easier."

"Abraham, please don't make me feel like a traitor. You

want to blame me for this. You want to have someone, some scapegoat for your hate. He's right, you know. There is a lot of hate in you. Even in you, Rabbi Abraham Cohen."

"And in you?"

"In me, too."

"Is this perhaps your way of getting back at me for 'controlling' you? I forbid you to speak of your Mormonism with my son, so you invite a beautiful Mormon girl his own age to the house, and let nature follow its course. You live your distorted religion through him, is that it?"

"No," she said, rubbing her temples. "You're making my head ache."

"And you, my heart!"

"You speak of tolerance, free will. Today, you realize that your boy is not going to come back when you say 'enough.' Today you see that he is going further and further away, back, even into our past. And you cannot tolerate it. You cannot abide it. You let him go and you bury me in your fury. Like the Nazis—"

"Stop, Sarah."

"Like the Nazis, who could not tolerate the Kaiser's defeat and found a scapegoat—or six million scapegoats—to bury in their anger. All in the name of the Master Race. You, of course, are no Nazi. No member of the Master Race. Only of the Chosen People. Read your scriptures, Abraham. I'm going to my room. I have the worst headache I've had in years."

Abraham called her as she left. "Wait."

She stopped but did not face him.

"A wife should not address her husband in such tones," he said.

"I apologize."

"The woman was given unto the man to be a helpmeet to him."

"I wish you still had the woman who was given to you. I wish you still had Deborah. I am certain she was everything that I am not." She heard the sofa creak as Abraham arose. He came to her, put his arm around her shoulders.

"Deborah was soft," he said. "She could not have survived much longer than she did. You are stubborn, proud, defiant, and sometimes very rude. You always have been. And Israel needs all kinds. Despite my harsh words, Sarah—not all un-deserved—you are my wife, my companion, even my helpmeet, and I love you."

She let herself fall into his arms, and returned his embrace, murmuring, "Forgive me."

"Of course," he said. "I have much to learn yet, and I am growing old. Sometimes, an old person is grumpy. Sometimes you are grumpy, too. Sometimes you say things you should not say to your husband. Sometimes I say things I should not say to my wife. And Isaac is the best and worst of both of us. But we must have faith. Perhaps, perhaps Hamburg will awaken his loyalties. Perhaps Hamburg will return him to us. Perhaps God has heard my prayers and is restoring my son to me in His own time, in His own way."

Sarah held him.

For a long time, Isaac walked up Woodward Boulevard, praying. The evening was cool. It had rained briefly in the after-noon and the air was humid and fragrant. A film of sweat cooled his forehead. His legs moved rapidly, automatically; his arms swung at his sides. He was not used to praying in such an active state, and the thing he prayed for—inner peace—seemed contrary to his movement. Still, he prayed. He had been taught to sway as he prayed, to catch the Hebrew rhythm with his body and use it to convey the message of the words, or to fill his body with the prayer. It had been a long time since he had prayed like that. The prayer he offered now seemed energized like the prayers of his boyhood, but not peaceful. And peace was what he wanted.

He stopped at a park and watched a pair of swans and three ducks floating on a murky pond. The breeze played with his hair. Night was coming. The park would not be safe after dark. But he was too agitated to leave yet. He tried to think of Elsa; her image was confused with his mother's.

One of the swans fluffed its feathers and seemed to look right at him. It was at peace. What cares did it have?

"Peace," Isaac repeated, and thought of the words of Jesus when he visited his disciples after his resurrection—the disciples who would all suffer for his cause. The words, likely the normal Hebrew greeting, translated into English with more than normal meaning: "Peace be unto you."

He thought of Joseph Smith, on his way to Carthage. "I go as a lamb to the slaughter, yet I am as calm as a summer's morning."

In the face of their trials, these men had known peace.

"Peace," he repeated, then prayed for something more. "Bless my father. Bless Abraham. Give him peace. My father needs peace."

# CHAPTER 25

His farewell was simple. Neither of his parents attended, and they were especially quiet when he got home. He knew they had been discussing him.

"You've had supper, I guess," his mother said.

"Yes."

"Good. No more dishes then. You let me know if you get hungry, yes?"

"Sure."

His father picked up a newspaper. "Recession on the way," he said.

"Is it?"

"Unemployment up all over the world. Here. Germany has hit seven percent. That's a big number for Germany."

"I'm sure it is."

Abraham opened the paper, moving his lips as he read. Isaac went to his room.

Two weeks later, in the Grubbe home, Isaac was set apart as a missionary. The next day, Abraham and Sarah took him to the airport. His destination: Salt Lake City, Utah. He would be endowed in the Salt Lake Temple and then go to Provo, to the Language Training Mission, where he would learn German.

Abraham was silent as they waited for boarding instructions. Sarah reminded Isaac to write and then slipped a photo of a house to him. "This was my home. If there is any way, see if it is still standing. I would like to know." Abraham glanced at her and folded his arms.

A flight attendant crossed in front of them. "It'll be just a moment," she said. Her hair was like Elsa's. Isaac looked around the airport to see if Elsa had appeared yet. He had counted on seeing her this one last time before he left.

"Flight 56, for Salt Lake City. Passengers with boarding passes may enter," the agent announced.

Isaac looked once more around the airport.

"You can board now, he says," Abraham stated.

"In a minute," said Isaac.

"You are waiting for something maybe? Someone maybe?"

"No — I mean yes. Of course. She has been my friend, Papa."

Then he saw her, standing by a glass door. She wiped her cheeks, blew him a kiss, and waved.

"Okay," he said, standing. "Guess it's time."

His mother kissed him. His father shook his hand. "We're always here if you need us," he said.

"Thank you. I know. Good-bye. I'll write."

Looking down, he boarded the plane.

When Isaac arrived from Salt Lake City, Provo was patched with autumn. The tops of the mountains were tinged yellow and rust. The foothills were pink—bright pink, like flamingo wings.

Isaac stepped off the bus and into the Amanda Knight building, which would be his home for the next two months. His name had been replaced by the title "Elder." Elder Cohen. He looked like all the other elders in the LTM: short hair, white shirt and tie, dark trousers. They were all partway processed dolls in this missionary factory.

His companion, Elder Gunther, from Richfield, Utah, was a strapping boy with gleaming brown hair and green eyes. He shook Isaac's hand firmly when they were introduced. Isaac imagined Gunther's hand had milked a lot of cows to be so strong.

The two talked for fifteen minutes that night, after lights-out. That was long enough for Elder Gunther to bear his testimony more than once and explain how his mission call had come as no surprise—he had felt impressed back in the seventh grade to study German. He asked Isaac if his call had come as a surprise.

Isaac answered, "Yes. Quite a surprise."


German lessons began the next day. Many of the words were Yiddish cognates. But German was definitely a foreign language. Foreign. Hard. Harsh. The language of the Nazis. This was how they said "No Jews Allowed": *"Juden Verboten."* "My struggle": *"Mein Kampf."*

Elder Gunther passed off all six discussions the first day of class. He had arranged to get a copy of the discussions at the beginning of the summer. He had memorized them all.

Beautifully. Elder Gunther suggested that Isaac should pray more fervently to be able to learn the language of his mission.

On the third morning, the cafeteria served bacon and eggs. Isaac had never tasted bacon. Even after his baptism he had maintained a kosher diet.

He stared at the fried meat on his plate. He could smell its blend of salty spices. It made him feel faint.

The other missionaries were bent over their breakfast plates — much as they would later be bent over their scriptures. They wolfed the food. Isaac watched them and looked at his own food.

The grease of the bacon was inextricable with the meat of the egg. He knew he would either leave his kosher customs this morning or go hungry until lunch — which would probably be ham.

He bit into his breakfast roll. The juices of his mouth and stomach welled. He moved the bacon with his fork.

"You don't like bacon?" asked Elder Gunther. Isaac shook his head. With greasy fingers, Elder Gunther picked up the bacon and shoved it into his own mouth. "Love bacon," he said, his mouth full of it.

"You're welcome," muttered Isaac. He took a bite of his egg and tasted what he knew was forbidden food to the Jews: the grease of a pig.


The German did not get any easier. And Isaac found he disliked his companion. Disliked him intensely.

Elder Gunther: the perfect Mormon. Raised in the faith, doubting nothing, questioning nothing, repeating fervently the words he knew his parents and leaders wanted to hear him say. People like Elder Gunther, thought Isaac, could march in a glorious parade, singing the anthems of their own praise, and trample anything or anybody in their way. The more Isaac thought about it, the more he disliked his companion. The more he disliked his companion, the harder the German became. The harder the German became, the more Elder Gunther goaded him by bearing his testimony. And it seemed that whenever Isaac reached desperation, the cafeteria served ham for lunch.

After a month in the LTM, Isaac had passed off only one discussion—and that with difficulty. Elder Gunther suggested to him that perhaps he had a learning disability, and added, "You'll need to pray real hard to overcome a problem like that."

Isaac glared at him.

One day each week, the companions usually went to downtown Provo. Isaac wrote to Elsa and to his parents. Elder Gunther wrote to the six girls who were waiting for him and usually dropped a note to his parents as well, probably to let them know he was everything they had ever hoped he would be.

The crisis came when Isaac tried—and failed—to pass off his second discussion. He began walking to his room. Elder Gunther said, "You are really going to have to pray harder, Elder Cohen. Do you want me to pray for you?"

Isaac stopped, looked his companion hard in the eyes, and slugged him.

Elder Gunther lurched over, groaning, then abruptly stood upright and flung his arm at Isaac's shoulders. Isaac dodged and hit him again. This time, the farm boy lunged for him, knocking him easily to the floor, and pinned him. In Elder Gunther's eyes shone triumph.

Isaac cursed him as other missionaries gathered and separated them. One of the German teachers approached and asked reproachfully how the fight had started.

"I hate him," muttered Isaac. "He's been pushing me since day one."

Elder Gunther tried to look humble as he answered, "I'm sorry it came to this. I hope I didn't hurt you, Elder. But it was just righteous indignation. Honest," he said, turning to the teacher, "I don't know what happened. I was just telling him he needed to pray harder and he hauls off and slugs me. But I couldn't let him beat me up, so I pinned him. Hope I didn't hurt you, Elder Cohen."

Isaac growled from deep in his throat.

He was called in to his branch president's office that evening.

President Rhobuck, a white-haired, grandfatherly man, smiled tenderly all the time he spoke to Isaac. "Now, what seems to be the problem?" he said.

Isaac bowed his head. His face grew hot.

"I understand that you and Elder Gunther are having some difficulties in your companionship."

"Yes."

"Can you tell me about it?"

"There's nothing to tell. I can't stand him, that's all."

"Do you have a reason to dislike him?"

"No. Yes—I don't know. Probably not. It's just that he—while I'm trying to learn German—he reminds me of—President Rhobuck, I'm a Jew."

"All right. Go on."

"For me to even consider learning German was a great—well, a great treachery, I guess. My parents were in concentration camps in Nazi Germany. They won't speak German. At least my father won't. My mother probably would if she had to, but she doesn't out of respect for my father. My father is a rabbi."

"My goodness. And you joined the Church on your own?"

"Yes."

"And you were called to Germany."

"Hamburg. The very city my parents lived in before the war. The very city!"

"Well, now, that's certainly interesting, isn't it. The Lord must know you very well to have given you such a call. Now, how can I help you approach this important mission in the spirit the Lord wants you to have?"

Isaac answered softly. "It's hard for me to have the right kinds of feelings for Elder Gunther. He reminds me of—forgive me, President—of the Nazis. It's like he wants to batter me with his testimony. I've suffered for mine. I've bled from my soul for it. Elder Gunther—he's a sponge. A sponge! He's soaked up the doctrine his parents have poured on him, and now he's squeezing it out over me. He acts like his testimony and mine can be measured by how easily we pass off the discussions. He learned his discussions before even coming to the LTM. And I—it's hard for me to make German sounds. It's hard for me to speak the language the Nazis used when they killed my grandparents and my uncles and aunts. It's hard."

President Rhobuck leaned back in his chair and nodded. "I can feel the difficulty you're in, Elder. I appreciate it. But I'm certain the Lord knew you would have these feelings. Part of your mission is to resolve them, I'd say."

"I know that."

"I feel impressed to tell you that what you are feeling now is only the beginning. You will feel this conflict even more than you do now. You will have to go to the depths of your soul to resolve it. But God is with you, son. He won't abandon you, though He will allow you to abandon Him, if you choose."

"I won't."

"I know you won't, Elder. I know you won't." The president stood and offered his hand. "Learn to love Elder Gunther," he said, reaching for the doorknob.

"I'll try," said Isaac.

"Don't try, Elder. Love. If you don't have enough love, then ask God for a loan. He doesn't charge interest."

"Yes, President," said Isaac. "I won't let you down."

President Rhobuck smiled again and opened the door.

The talk inspired Isaac to pray more fervently, but it didn't erase his disdain for his companion. Nor did it make the German easier.

Still, by the end of the week, he passed off his second discussion. He suspected nothing would be easy for him on his mission. But at least in Germany he would get a new companion.


Hamburg, when the group of missionaries arrived, was decked out for Christmas. Christmas trees glowed behind frosted store windows as the elders traveled to the mission home. Isaac scanned the tidy streets. He was looking for the house: the house which had sheltered his mother's childhood and given refuge to both his parents after the war. He knew he would recognize it, and he knew he would find it eventually. He was certain so important a house could not have been destroyed. Of course, the address would be different. Hamburg had been overhauled since the war. But the house would be there, and he would know it.

# CHAPTER 26

In Michigan, Rabbi Abraham Cohen addressed an athletic convention attended by several hundred Olympic hopefuls. He spoke about the war and the death camps briefly but mostly talked about the responsibility the athletes had to be ambassadors of peace. "Would that the whims of the world's demagogues could be played out on the soccer field and not the battlefield. The football makes a very bad, noisy transition to its shrunken cousin the hand grenade."

The athletes gave him a standing ovation after the speech, and many surged to meet him. He noticed a slight, fawnlike girl who seemed content to wait for the crowds to disperse before coming forward. When only a handful of people lingered around him, the girl stepped up. "Rabbi Cohen, my name is Annie Gold. My Hebrew name is Channa. I am a gymnast. I would like to talk to you."

Abraham shook her hand and said, "Shalom, Channa."

Channa became a frequent visitor to the Cohen household. She had hundreds of questions for the rabbi, about the religion they shared, about the war against the Jews, about fascism and pacifism.

Abraham could not help but think of Channa as a wife for Isaac. But he did not mention his son to the girl until she asked about him. There was a picture of Isaac, taken the day of his Bar Mitzvah, in Abraham's study. Channa pointed to it and said, "Your son?"

"Yes," said Abraham.

"He is dead?"

"Physically he is alive. In other ways, he is dead. He left the faith."

Sarah was present, too—a married man would never be alone with a single girl in a righteous home. She cleared her throat.

"Your son left the faith," Channa repeated.

Sarah nodded as Abraham said, "He converted."

Channa's hands came to her mouth and muffled her exclamation.

"He is a Mormon missionary in Germany," said Abraham, looking at Sarah.

"Rabbi—a Mormon—in Germany!"

He nodded, still looking at his wife. "Perhaps, Channa, when you are at the Olympics in Munich—perhaps you might like to call my son, or try to talk to him. I would like you to meet my son. I would like that very much."

"Why don't you come to the Olympics too, Rabbi—you and Mrs. Cohen. Why don't you come, and we'll all talk to your son."

"Go back there? Come, Channa!"

"A lot of Jews who were in the camps are planning a pilgrimage."

"Yes, I know. I know about it. A pilgrimage back to Hell."

"No. To remembrance. To remind us all of what happened."

"Yes, yes, of course," said Abraham. "I understand that. Of course we must remember. Of course. Many have only good motives for the journey back there. Others, though, are seeking to write books with themselves as heroes. I do not wish to be a member of their dramas."

"But you were there, Rabbi! And you, Mrs. Cohen. Don't you have an obligation to us who were not there, to tell us everything, to keep the camps burning in our minds now and throughout history?"

Sarah intoned, "Not back there," as Abraham said, "Channa, you are so full of life and conviction, tiny though you are. You are a little warrior. We need more like you."

"Think about going to Germany," said Channa. "Both of you. Think about it."

"We will, Channa," said Abraham. "Of course we will."

Two weeks later, Rabbi Abraham and Mrs. Sarah Cohen were formally invited to participate in a pilgrimage back to Germany and to Auschwitz, Poland, with other Jews who had been imprisoned there. They discussed it together. Sarah found that the thought of Germany made her tired. Nonetheless, they decided to go back. Back, for a moment, to Egypt.

But not for help. Never for help.


Isaac received frequent letters from his parents, but Elsa's letters were the brightest moments of his weeks. Hers were so vibrant and full of love, though gradually they became less and less romantic. When she enrolled at BYU, her letters became quite businesslike, though still delightful and distinctly hers. Occasionally, she mentioned a young man named Mark Dearden, whom she said she "hung out" with occasionally. The name, after it was mentioned five times in as many letters, became threatening. Isaac thought seriously one evening about what he would do if Elsa were to write him a "Dear John." Would he finish his mission? Or would he fly home to remind her of what they had, to try to keep her from committing eternal treachery?

He had converted to Mormonism independently and had independently accepted his mission call. Still, this was not his mission alone; it was THEIR mission. His and Elsa's. If she were to withdraw from it, it would be half a mission. Yes, it would be tempting to leave Germany if Elsa left him. But he would not, could not do it. He could not capitulate so easily. The Lord, not Elsa, had called him. Whatever she did, Isaac would finish his mission. He recommitted himself to that end in prayer—the day before the letter came.

Somehow, he knew what it was just from looking at the envelope:

Dear, dear Isaac,
I don't know how to say what I need to say to you. Please, please try to understand. Please, never doubt my love for you, because I purely love you, now and always.
When you joined the Church, you broke the heart of the man you love better than any other man on earth: your father. But you had to do it because—because you had to do it. You had to do what you felt was right even if it hurt someone you loved so much. A person has to choose his or her own way. You and I both know that.

Isaac, Mark has asked me to marry him. I've accepted. We haven't set a date yet. I don't know.

Please, please forgive me for hurting you like this. I couldn't stand for you to hate me. I could never stand that, because, oh Isaac, I'm not lying when I say I still love you. Please respect that love, and this decision.

Yours truly,

Elsa


Isaac took a pen, crossed out "Yours truly," wrote "his truly," added a note ("if it's what you want"), and mailed the letter back to Elsa.

It hurt. How it hurt! In the pit of his stomach, behind his eyes, around his heart, it hurt. He did not talk about it to anyone.

He went through four months and two companions numbly and with no success as a missionary. He found it difficult to be excited about anything—until one day when he and his companion were biking up a strange street and Isaac saw the house. His mother's house.

He stopped cold. That was it. He knew it was. It was old and rickety and had peeling paint and looked out of place in tidy Hamburg. But it was the house. Here were his roots. Here was the house of refuge. His parents' sanctuary.

The missionaries had an appointment, so he could not stay at the house. But he memorized its address and promised himself he would return to it. Soon.

# CHAPTER 27

Isaac's next transfer was to a small suburb of Hamburg. His assigned companion: Elder Gunther.

Isaac hoped—even prayed—that Elder Gunther was some new, fresh-from-Provo kid who knew nothing about anything. Not the Elder Gunther of the LTM. But he knew exactly who his companion was.

Elder Gunther.

Elder Gunther gave Isaac a firm handshake and said, "Long time no see."

Isaac grunted an unintelligible response. Already, his stomach was tensing.

"So, how's your German?" asked Gunther.

"*Gut*," said Isaac.

"I've had fifteen baptisms. How about you?"

Isaac was tempted to say, "Twenty-three, but who's counting?" But he knew the lie would catch up with him. "One," he answered, wondering whether his first baptism—a sixteen-year-old girl named Hilde Braun—had been baptized for any other reason than her infatuation with him and whether she was still active.

"Just one, huh? You'll have to pray harder, Elder."

Isaac smiled drolly. "You betcha."

His prayers had not been too effective of late, he thought. Elder Gunther had turned out to be Elder Gunther.

After a week of tracting, Isaac could understand why his companion had had fifteen baptisms in a mission where elders were lucky to find two or three "golden contacts." Elder Gunther battered his contacts with his testimony. It was as simple as that. Undoubtedly, surmised Isaac, the fifteen "converts" had accepted the only visible escape from the elder's relentless badgering: baptism. At least if they did what he wanted, he would let them alone.

But with Isaac present, the principle seemed to fail. Few people even permitted them in their doors. Elder Gunther blamed Isaac for the difficulties and advised him to "pray harder."

Isaac did pray harder—for a different companion.

During their second week together, they met a group of anti-Mormons, who eagerly shared their literature with them.

The bitter tirades against the Church hardly affected Isaac. He had had a lifetime of experience in religious prejudice and had already read anti-Mormon literature (that which his father had discreetly placed on his bed). He shrugged them off.

Elder Gunther took them as a personal affront and tried, rather illogically, to refute their claims.

Three weeks later, Elder Gunther received a telegram. His father had been killed in a car accident. The driver of the other car had been drunk. Elder Gunther did not speak for two days.

Early the third morning after the telegram came, Isaac awakened to find Gunther reading the anti-Mormon pamphlets with a flashlight.

"What are you doing?" Isaac asked.

Elder Gunther's head shot up guiltily. He dropped the pamphlet.

Isaac switched on the light. "Elder?" he said.

A blush was settled deep in Gunther's shiny cheeks. He was panting.

"Come on, Elder, what's up?" Isaac's tone sounded callous, even to himself.

Gunther shook his head.

"You confused?"

Gunther shook his head again, frantically, then bowed it. His arms relaxed at his sides.

"You're confused."

Gunther nodded.

"Go ahead and talk, Elder. I'm listening."

"No."

"Go on. It's all right. Talk."

"It's just—my dad. His patriarchal blessing said he would have a long life. He was only fifty-two."

"Yeah. It hurts to lose him, I know."

"It didn't come true!"

"The blessing, you mean?"

"Yes. It didn't come true!"

"Elder, did you want God to conform to man's system of time?"

"What do you know, Cohen? What do you understand?"

"Some."

"You don't understand jack. You don't understand God or nothing."

"No one understands God. No mortal can. All we can do is begin to be like Him. All we can do is understand him as we come to understand ourselves."

"I don't understand God," moaned Elder Gunther.

"God doesn't fit into a neat little packet, Elder, any more than you or I do."

"I've never seen this anti-Mormon stuff. Have you?"

"Some."

"I've never heard of—of all the stuff they say about us."

Isaac shrugged. "Probably some of it's true. And some of it's false. But most of it is just bitter. That should tell you something about its source."

"Bear me your testimony, Elder Cohen. Please. Please bear me your testimony."

Isaac knelt by Elder Gunther but did not look at him. "I never wanted to believe in the Church," began Isaac. "My testimony came like—I don't know—like a pearl in a stolen oyster. A priceless pearl. The gospel is true. It is. Jesus is the Christ. He lives. Your father lives, too, Elder Gunther." Isaac's voice broke. "I'm just—just Isaac Cohen. I'm no one special, Elder. What can I say to you?"

"My dad had a real strong testimony."

"I'm sure he did."

Elder Gunther blinked his eyes wildly and burst into quaking sobs. Isaac was filled with a strange mix of pity and love for him. He held out his arms as his own father had done so often for him when he was hurt or confused. Elder Gunther threw himself into them and clung. Isaac whispered, "*Shah, shah*. It's all right." His own tears flowed onto Elder Gunther's head.

The next morning, Elder Gunther did not mention the incident except to say thanks. But a new friendship existed between them now. They both knew it.

On their diversion day, Isaac suggested they go sightseeing. Elder Gunther agreed. Isaac, on his bicycle, took the lead and steered toward the old house that had been his parents' refuge.

"Where are we going?" called Elder Gunther.

"Just follow me," Isaac called back.

A skinny old woman was sitting on the porch, knitting. She eyed the elders hard and shook her head.

"Excuse me," said Isaac.

She frowned at him, shook her head once more, and turned with forced concentration to her knitting.

"My name is Isaac Cohen," he said.

The woman raised one threatening brow.

"My mother was raised in this home. Both my parents lived here after the war."

"Cohen," she said in a low, unemotional tone. "Your parents were Jews?"

"They still are."

"Of course they are."

"Of course," repeated Isaac.

Elder Gunther parked his bike and stepped towards the woman. "Elder Gunther," he said with a slight bow.

The woman narrowed her eyes at him, then at Elder Cohen. "You are a missionary?" she said.

Elder Gunther answered in his near fluent German, "Of

The Church of Jesus Christ of Latter-day Saints. We have a message for you, if you would care to hear it."

She kept her eyes on Isaac. "You are a convert?" she asked. Isaac nodded.

"I am Frau Elen Sell. You may come in." She stood.

Elder Gunther followed eagerly. Isaac, tense and tight-lipped, hesitated, and then he followed too.

The first thing Isaac noticed as he stepped into the parlor was a fancy-cut mirror above a mantle. In front of the mirror was a photograph of a soldier.

The woman watched Isaac's eyes. "My husband," she said. "He fought in the war."

"Which war?" asked Elder Gunther.

The woman watched Isaac. "The last war. He was wounded in Poland and left for dead in Russia. But he survived. He was luckier than most. My parents died here in Hamburg. Burned to death in the bomb raids."

"Millions of people died in the war. Millions of people were burned to death," murmured Isaac.

"Yes," answered Frau Sell.

"Is your husband here?" asked Elder Gunther.

"My husband is always here. In bed. He was paralyzed from the neck down during the war."

"I'm sorry to hear that," said Elder Gunther.

Frau Sell pointed to a door. "He's in there, if you would like to meet him." She faced Elder Cohen. "Would you like to meet my husband?"

He nodded.

Still watching him, her expression unchanging, she opened the door.

Her husband, a pale lump of flesh with a wide-open mouth,

was lying under a flowery sheet. He opened one blue eye and groaned a question as the missionaries entered the room.

"These are missionaries," said the woman. "Christian missionaries. This one is Elder Gunther. This one is Elder Cohen. Elder Cohen's parents used to live here."

The man's other eye fluttered spastically. "Cohen," he repeated.

A chill ran up Isaac's back.

"He is a convert," the woman said. "A convert to this religion they're preaching."

The old man grunted again.

"Perhaps, if you have a moment, we might tell you about our church," offered Elder Gunther.

At this, the man laughed. "A moment," he said. "A moment. I have forever. No place to go. No legs to take me there."

Elder Gunther began with the Joseph Smith story.

Isaac said nothing. Even when Elder Gunther asked him if he wanted to pray, he shook his head. "You do it," he said.

The missionaries scheduled a second discussion with Frau and Herr Sell.

Isaac could not justify or explain even to himself his feelings toward this man and woman who had taken the home where his mother and uncles and grandparents had once been a happy family, and where his parents had found refuge. The woman, too skinny, her hair dull gray, lips dry, eyes magnified by blue, tortoiseshell glasses — this woman was the opposite of his soft mother. This woman was an imposter and an interloper, pretending that Sarah's house was hers. And the man, like death itself, a restless apparition between inappropriate, springtime sheets — he was the opposite of Abraham. He was hard, stubborn, sarcastic. A shriveled soul in a too-fleshy body, so full of itself as to be immobile. Abraham, by contrast, was a full soul in a shriveled shell.

Isaac had no desire to return to the house. But he did return the following week, as duty demanded. Without any embellishment, he gave the discussion on the plan of salvation.

Frau Sell agreed to hear the next discussion. Isaac, heaving a sigh, set a date and time for it.

But, as it turned out, the next discussion did not concern the Church. Instead the Sells talked about the war.

Herr Sell reminisced about standing at attention every morning and listening as part of *Mein Kampf* was read. Some of the young men, he said, giggled during these solemn moments and were summarily punished. He himself never laughed, he claimed. "Perhaps I do not agree with Hitler's ideas now, but then — then, Hitler was the Führer. One owes respect to one's leader, whoever that leader is," he said.

Elder Gunther mechanically quoted the twelfth Article of Faith: "We believe in being subject to kings, presidents, rulers, and magistrates, and in obeying, honoring, and sustaining the law."

A coldness welled in Isaac. He glared at his companion. "How long do you 'obey, honor and sustain'?" he asked. "Until your leader, whoever he is, destroys your family and then begins to pick away at your soul?" The German flowed easily. His voice was hate frosted.

Elder Gunther stammered an unintelligible reply, which Isaac cut short by saying, "Hitler was a murderer and a devil. May his name and soul burn slowly in the lowest, hottest pit of Hell." Had he been in Michigan, he would have spit. Here, the saliva only welled under his tongue, contaminated by the filthy name.

No one spoke until Herr Sell said, "Of course, we all feel

guilty—for what happened. But the future should not be held hostage by mistakes of the past."

Isaac stood. "Mistakes! You talk of the massacre of MY FAMILY as some unfortunate accident. Like spilling milk on the breakfast table. Well, it was no accident and it was no milk. It was blood that was spilled. Blood!" The vessels in his neck bulged.

"As the blood of Jesus Christ was spilled by the Jews," said Frau Sell softly, wearing a lemony smile.

"The Jews did not kill Jesus," breathed Isaac. "The Romans killed him. The Romans!"

The quadriplegic spoke. "Elder Cohen, what does it matter to you? You are a convert. You have—what you call—a 'testimony.'"

"Of Messiah," cried Isaac. "The Messiah of MY people! He was one of us. He was a Jew! He came to us, for us, to fulfill the covenants of God to Abraham. You—all of you—are gentiles. Messiah would never have come to you if he hadn't come to us first. You think God approved of the Holocaust because the Jews betrayed Jesus and allowed the Romans to kill him? You think God approved? The Romans were Gentiles, too. They were doing the work of the devil when they crucified the anointed one. And the Nazis, every one of them, were doing the work of the devil when they murdered the chosen ones. Every one, EVERY ONE of them was doing the work of the devil." These last words he directed to the paralyzed man.

Elder Gunther suggested that they reschedule their appointment. Frau Sell agreed to let them return the following day. Isaac said nothing, and the missionaries awkwardly left.

Isaac could not sleep that night. He wanted to go home.

Home to *challah* bread on Sabbath eve. Home to where his father was wrapped in his tallith—his prayer shawl. Home to big cars and English and streets and sites he knew. Home to nice people. Home to Elsa.

His mind traveled to the temple. The house of the Lord. Home.

When Judas Maccabeus had restored the Jews their temple, only a little oil was present to light the holy place. Yet the Lord had made it sufficient.

Isaac sat silently on his bed. It was so dark. He wanted to pray but could not. It was too dark. The darkness itself seemed to be a presence. All around him. Cold. Black. Demonic. "Please Father," he whispered, "help me pray. Help me. Give me a prayer to say." Again he waited. "Please, God, help me. The darkness—please, God, I miss my home so much. Please, Father in Heaven, make my light sufficient to take me home. It is so dark here and I am so lost, so alone. There is such hate here. Such hate! Please, God." He prayed for nearly two hours. Prayed, and thought about his father.

Abraham had not spoken to him much of the Holocaust. But someone had once told Isaac of what his father had suffered. He could remember the man's words clearly: "Your father bought your freedom at a high price. Can you imagine watching your friends, your brothers, enter a gas chamber? Can you imagine it? And can you imagine having to remove their bodies after the poison has done its work? Can you imagine losing all your friends, your wife, your child, your parents? Can you?"

Isaac had cried then and asked his father about the terrible story later that day. His father had silently nodded.

As he thought about his father now, he imagined the emaciated prisoners of Auschwitz. He imagined one of them with his father's eyes. He hated, hated, hated the Nazis for doing that to his father.

The war was still going on within Isaac. It, too, was part of his heritage.

He prayed again in the morning, and once more as he approached the Sell house.

Frau Sell opened the door and smiled her sour smile. Isaac tensed. He prayed again to be able to feel peace in this, his parents' home.

He looked around himself. It seemed he could hear children singing. It seemed he could see a young girl eating chocolate. A young girl who had been Sarah.

He taught the Sells about the principles of repentance and forgiveness and asked them to read the Book of Mormon.

The next week, Isaac fasted before the scheduled meeting with the Sells. He prayed to be able to see the couple as God saw them. When they went to the old house, he tried to imagine Frau Sell as a little girl—much as he had imagined Sarah—a life full of dreams before her, and Herr Sell as an anxious, ambulatory child filled with impossible plans. For a moment, he felt he could love them. But abruptly, another vision swallowed the first: hundreds of children who had also had dreams and plans and fantasies, waiting in line for the gas chamber marked "Showers." The beginnings of love withered within him, and he taught what he considered to be a stale lesson. But he dreamt of the Sells that night. He could not remember much of the dream upon awakening, only that they had been dressed in white, and he had loved them. He heard a voice: "Forgive them, for they know not what they do." The words were vivid in his mind as the alarm buzzed.

"Elder Gunther," Isaac called, "I need your help."

Elder Gunther stirred. "Sure, Elder."

"I need to pray harder. Would you help me? Would you pray with me, please?"

Elder Gunther slid from his bed to the floor on his knees. Isaac prayed beside him, asking for a loan of love.

"I wouldn't worry about the Sells if I were you," said Elder Gunther afterwards. "I don't think they'll convert or anything."

"It's not the Sells I'm worried about."


They visited the Sells later that day. Isaac took six yellow rosebuds and asked Frau Sell to put them in water in her husband's room and watch them blossom. She smiled almost like a young woman as she admitted, "My husband and I—we both love roses very much."

The next time the missionaries visited, Frau Sell gave them fresh-baked bread.

# CHAPTER 28

Sarah breathed in deeply as she stepped off the jet. The German air had recovered from its putridity. It smelled now of industry: hot tar, sulphur, coal, wood. The airline hostesses directed the passengers towards huge signs of five intertwined circles above the title, "München 1972."

Back in Hamburg.

Sarah straightened her hat and turned to Abraham, who was just behind her. She was struck by how much Abraham resembled a vague, pale, wrinkled memory: Rav Hillel. She put her hand on his elbow. But Abraham's eyes did not meet hers. They widened and focused brightly on something to Sarah's distant left. His mouth quivered and spread to a half smile. "There he is," he whispered.

Sarah turned and saw Isaac. She held her arms open as he ran to her. "You're so big," she said, embracing him. "So much bigger than I remember."

"And you are more lovely than I remember, Mama."

"Nonsense," she said, taking his face in her hands. "Truth is, I'm bigger than you remember as well. I've gained twelve pounds. Twelve pounds, Isaac! My face is as round and wrinkled as an old pumpkin."

"You are beautiful," Isaac said, kissing her fingertips. He turned to his father.

For a moment, neither said anything. Abraham swallowed, nodded slowly, and waited. Isaac breathed, "Father," and extended his hand. Abraham shook it.

A shy, well-dressed young man approached. He introduced himself as Elder Gunther, Isaac's companion. He also extended his hand for the rabbi and Sarah to shake.

The four of them went to lunch in the hotel where Sarah and Abraham had made arrangements to stay for their interlude in Hamburg before flying to Munich and the Olympics. Conversation was anything but flowing. A tangible tension was pervasive. Abraham said only a few words. Sarah's conversation with Elder Gunther lagged and sputtered and then yielded to awkward silence.

Isaac broke the silence by asking, "How is Elsa? Happily married, I hope."

Sarah and Abraham exchanged a glance. Sarah stammered. "I bring you her greetings. She is — I believe she is happy, yes."

"Her husband treats her all right?" Isaac asked.

"She broke her engagement," blurted Sarah, as Abraham loudly cleared his throat.

Isaac shook his head and expelled a single laugh. "Please pass the water," he said. "I'm awful thirsty."

Abraham passed it, commenting, "You have put on some weight, Isaac. Not too much, of course. It looks good. You look like a man now, not a little boy. You look good. Very good."

"He does," Sarah agreed.

Isaac nodded distractedly. "I've gained ten pounds. All muscle, I'm sure."

Elder Gunther laughed and said, "Absolutely."

Isaac sipped his water and ate some salad. He sighed. Sarah put her hand on his. He shook his head. "She must really hate me. She didn't even write to tell me that—the last letter I got from her—"

"Don't worry about it," said Sarah, squeezing his fingers. "Let it rest."

"I'm not worried. It just makes me sad. She was a friend, after all."

"I know."

Again, Abraham cleared his throat. "There is a girl, a good girl, on the team here. A gymnast. I think maybe you should meet her. Maybe you might like her."

"Abraham," whispered Sarah, "you know these boys, these missionaries—they can't even think about girls now."

The rabbi's eyes widened. "Not even think about them? You think God is going to tell two young, handsome men in the prime of life that they shouldn't think about girls?" He faced Isaac. "This God you serve—he tells you not to think about girls?"

Isaac squirmed. His companion grinned. "We can think about girls," said Isaac. "Just not do anything. We are under covenant to keep ourselves chaste."

"Chastity is one thing. That is a decision—a good one. But thoughts, they are something else again. Part of being a man is recognizing and purely appreciating the beauty of a woman. So you can think about girls, then."

Isaac shrugged. "Yes."

"Good. This girl, her name is Annie. Channa is her Hebrew

name. She is lovely. You might want to meet her and think about her."

Now Sarah cleared her throat.

"If she's with the Olympics, she's in Munich. That's outside the Hamburg mission," Isaac explained.

"Maybe you could get permission," said Abraham. "Or maybe she will be on television. Or maybe you could write to her, and I could take her the letter. She is not only beautiful, this girl, but intelligent and conservative too. A good Jewish girl. A girl I would be proud to have for a daughter."

"Abraham!" scolded Sarah.

"You can think about girls, then," repeated the old man.

"Yes, Papa."

They finished their meal. At the hotel door, Isaac hugged his mother and once more, awkwardly, shook his father's hand. As he turned to leave, his mother pressed a letter into his palm. She kissed his cheek and whispered, "From her."

The exchange did not go unnoticed by Abraham, who stood for a long moment staring at the envelope in his son's hand. He glanced at Sarah. "Good to meet you," he said stiffly to Elder Gunther and then bowed. "Isaac," he said, turning, "you look well." He waited for Sarah, who kissed Isaac once more on both his cheeks.

"That was a letter from the Grubbe girl, I presume," said Abraham as he and Sarah entered their hotel suite.

"I had lunch with her last week," said Sarah. "I told you that."

"You didn't tell me she gave you a letter. And you didn't tell me you were going to give it to Isaac."

"You didn't ask."

Abraham sat on the bed and raised his arms. "Why lift the boy's hopes?" he sighed. "If this girl had been serious about him in the first place, you think another man could have made her forget him?"

"She broke her engagement with the other man."

"Why are you so loyal to this girl?"

"Why do you hate her so much?"

"Hate her? I don't hate her. I don't hate anyone." He pointed his finger at Sarah. "You accused me of hatred once before, and I thought deeply about it. I asked the Almighty to purify my heart, cleanse my mind. He answered my prayer. Even here, even in this country, I do not hate. I ache, yes. But hate? No, Sarah. No more. I do not hate that girl. But I do not want her for Isaac."

"Perhaps you don't hate her, but she frightens you. You realize that she could keep your boy from returning to the dreams you—we—have for him."

He pursed his lips. "Perhaps that is true."

"I know you don't hate anyone," she said, sitting beside him on the bed and taking his hand. "Forgive me for suggesting it. But I know how hard it is for you to let your son choose his own road, to watch him walking away from you."

"It is hard," Abraham said, his eyes misting. "And, you see, Sarah, I can never give up hope that he will return to me."

"I know," Sarah said. She arose and looked out the hotel window. "So many memories here," she said. "Hamburg."

"So many memories," Abraham repeated.

"And not all bad ones. I remember a little school, not far from here—oh, I'm sure it's no longer standing—and a young, very ill-behaved girl who drew a rather uncomplimentary picture of her school principal and accidentally gave it to him with her assignment."

Abraham chuckled. "I remember the picture. Imagine that. I still remember it. It must have been very good. Very impressive."

"You told me that you and I seemed to be fated to know each other well," she said.

"I said that back then?"

"You meant that you would have to spend a lot of time correcting me. I was so very bad, you see."

"Ah yes. And so it has been. I have spent a lifetime correcting you."

She smiled at him. "And I you," she said, returning her eyes to the window. "Oh, Hamburg," she sighed, "how you have changed since last I saw you."

Abraham joined her at the window. "Hamburg," he breathed.


Isaac spoke only in monosyllables as he and Elder Gunther walked to their apartment.

"That girl was pretty special, huh," said Elder Gunther. "Was she the one you wrote to when we were in the LTM?"

Isaac nodded as they entered the apartment. "Yes. That's Elsa," he whispered as he sat on his bed. He stared at the letter.

"Well, open it!" Elder Gunther said.

Isaac glanced at him and slid his finger under the flap.

"Why don't you read it aloud?" suggested his companion.

Isaac gave him a threatening look and shook his head once, firmly. To himself he read:

Dear Isaac,

This is about the tenth letter I've started to you. I hope I can finish this one and get it off. I hear your folks may go to Germany for the Olympics. Maybe I can send it with your mom.

I feel so stupid, because I know you must think I'm disloyal, fickle, a lot of other things. Let me get right to the point. I've broken my engagement. You had nothing to do with my decision, and I certainly don't expect you to take me back. I do want you to know, though, that I never, not once, stopped loving you. I sobbed so hard the night I wrote you that "Dear John." My eyes were swollen for two days afterwards, I swear. I know it's stupid for me to tell you that, because the "Dear John" must have been a total shock to you, and it must have been so hard. I'm not begging you to take me back, but I do want you to know I miss you. You have been my best friend for so long. I'm not asking you to have me as your girlfriend, Isaac, but may I be your friend?

I want you to know how proud I am of you. Believe me, this wasn't any kind of a planned test of your faith—at least I didn't plan it—but if it had been, you would have passed with flying colors. There was always a little part of me that was really scared maybe you did join the Church just for me, and maybe if I left you, you might leave the Church. You really had to stand on your own, though, and you stood tall. That makes me happy. Really happy.

I am not the same Elsa you knew when you left. I've learned a lot. My ex-fiance taught me many things, mostly about myself, not all of which were pleasant to learn. I'm grateful to him for the things he helped me learn, but, again, I'm sorry my lessons had to cause you pain.

You don't have to write me back. I'll understand if you don't. Even if you don't want to be my friend after what I did to you, I remain,

Your friend,

Elsa

Isaac bowed his head and repeated her name.

"Good news?" asked Elder Gunther.

Isaac folded the letter and replaced it in its envelope. "Hope you've got some things to keep you busy, Elder," he said, "because I've got to write a long letter to my girlfriend."

# CHAPTER 29

A group of nearly one hundred former prisoners of the Nazis joined in a pilgrimage to Dachau and Auschwitz, television cameras accompanying them. Abraham and Sarah walked silently, tearlessly, together. They stood before the photos of shaven, starving Jews. They stared somberly at the monument engraved with a multilingual promise: Never Again.

Some of the pilgrims wept. A few sobbed loudly, painfully. But Sarah and Abraham were quiet, until softly, Abraham put his arm around his wife and recited Kaddish.

Sarah said then the names of her parents, brothers, friends, loved ones, lost ones. They whose mouths had been collectively silenced now had just hers to speak their names, to remember their individual lives and send the echoes of their being to God's ear:

"Papa: Aaron Samuel Sinasohn. Mama: Eva Weir Sinasohn. Brother: David Sinasohn, lion of my people. Brother: Moses Sinasohn, little lover of the word. Sister-in-law and friend: Zipporah Steinberg Sinasohn. Her children: Jacob, Samuel, and the baby I never saw, born and killed in captivity.

"I remember. I will not forget. I will not forget you!"

The Olympics were spectacular. Flags and flowers brightened the arenas; national anthems moved athletes to tears; people of all nations applauded a teary Russian gymnast named Olga Korbut.

Channa performed her routines beautifully, but her abilities paled beside those of Tourisheva, Olga Korbut, and America's own Kathy Rigby.

Television crews traveled from Olympic arenas to Olympic villages and the sights of Germany. They traveled back in time, too, to the 1936 Olympics and the victory of Jesse Owens under the disapproving eye of Adolf Hitler.

Abraham was sitting in an armchair watching the swimming competition on television in his Munich hotel room when broadcaster Jim Mackay interrupted the program with the announcement that Israel's athletes were being held hostage by unidentified masked terrorists.

Abraham groaned. Sarah, who had been reading on the bed, cried, "What is it? What?"

"Our boys," moaned Abraham. "They've taken our sons again." He gestured to the screen. Sarah watched the scene change from a troubled announcer to a common apartment building where armed, hooded men paced.

"What has happened?" she said.

Abraham motioned to the television. The voice of the

announcer said that as yet the terrorists and their cause were unidentified. There were rumors that they were neo-Nazis.

Abraham's face was expressionless. His brows were raised high, as though only by such effort could his eyes stay open. His jaw had dropped. Saliva gathered at the corners of his mouth.

The phone rang. Sarah turned to it and stopped breathing. She let it ring again and then tremulously answered. "Yes?"

It was Channa. "Mrs. Cohen," she said, "have you heard?"

"Are you all right, my dear?" said Sarah.

"They've given me a bodyguard, in case there's trouble."

"It's as though they were waiting for us," said Sarah. "Who knows where they've been hiding these past thirty years!"

"May I talk to the rabbi?"

Sarah gave the phone to her husband. "It's Channa."

"Hello," he said hoarsely, taking the phone but keeping his eyes focused on the television screen.

Channa's voice broke as she said, "Oh, Rabbi!"

"Shalom, Channa."

"Have you heard anything?" she managed. "Do you know who they are? Are they—Nazis?"

"Whoever they are," said the rabbi, "at heart, they are the same as the Nazis."

"I can't imagine it," she cried. "I'm so frightened!"

"Hush, child. You will be protected by the Americans."

"They could toss a bomb, fire a rifle. Besides, even if I am safe—what about them? What about the Israelis? Have you seen the news pictures?"

"Yes, yes."

"How could it happen?" she sobbed. "Where were the police? Where were the guards?"

"I'm sure this—thing—has been well planned. For years,

surely, they have planned it. For thirty years, perhaps, from the depths of Hell, they have planned it. Perhaps for two thousand years, from the depths of Hell, they have planned it."

"Are there guards at your hotel?"

"Don't worry about us."

"Please be careful, Rabbi."

"Yes. We will be careful. You be careful too."

"Of course."

Abraham hung up the phone. "She is a good girl," he said. "That she should have to see this! *Oy!*"

Sarah knelt beside her husband and put her head on his lap. They watched the drama progress, listened to the feeble commentaries of the newscasters.

The Olympic competition progressed almost as if nothing had happened, and eventually the television crews returned to their reports of the games, interrupting them every half-hour for the latest news on the hostage situation.

By evening it was known that the terrorists were not neo-Nazis, but Arabs, members of the Palestine Liberation Organization: The Black September.

For two days, Sarah and Abraham hardly left their room. They stayed near the television set. Channa called them several times a day with the latest rumors circulating among the athletes.

On the third day of terror, the Arabs killed their hostages when international forces attempted a rescue.

Abraham and Sarah numbly watched the death scene, watched the eleven young, athletic bodies being taken from their death chamber. Neither spoke.

Isaac heard the news on the radio at the Sells' house. Frau

Sell let him use their phone to call his parents in Munich, but when he heard his father's voice, he found he could not speak.

"We are going home," said Abraham to his son. "We will see you tomorrow at the Hamburg hotel, if your mission president will give you permission."

"Yes," Isaac said.

# CHAPTER 30

After the massacre, Isaac was sullen and withdrawn. Elder Gunther asked what was wrong. He could not answer. His parents came. The missionaries met them at the hotel. Abraham shook his son's hand.

"I thought you might like to meet some of our — well, our friends," said Isaac, "before you go home."

Abraham looked at his watch.

"Just for a minute," assured Isaac, his eyes locked on his mother. "Just for a minute."

They drove in the Cohens' rented Mercedes-Benz to the old house — the old refuge.

Abraham swayed as he stepped out of the car and recognized the place. Sarah took his hand. "Hello," she breathed.

"How did it survive?" whispered Abraham.

"Oh, my dear, how could it not have survived? It is much

too important a place! Too much beauty, too much pain was in this house. How could it crumble with such a foundation?"

"Who lives here now?" Abraham asked.

"A family," said Isaac, knocking on the door.

Frau Sell answered, smiled at Isaac and Elder Gunther, and then turned her eyes to Abraham and Sarah.

"My parents," said Isaac.

Sarah glanced at her husband. "This was my home," she said in German as Frau Sell invited them to enter.

Sarah's eyes circled the front room. Abraham found the picture of the bemedaled Herr Sell.

"Your son is a good boy," said Frau Sell. Abraham glanced at her and then returned to the picture.

"My husband," said Frau Sell, "would you like to meet him? He's disabled—he's in here." She opened the bedroom door and said loudly, "Elder Cohen's parents are here."

"You are Mormons too?" asked Herr Sell.

To this, Abraham spoke, in Yiddish. "God forbid!" He looked at his watch. "Let us go," he said. "We must go back."

The Cohens and missionaries exchanged obligatory niceties with the Sells and returned to the hotel. Sarah carried on a superficial conversation with Elder Gunther about how nice the house had been when she was a child, how badly it was in need of restoration. Abraham and Isaac did not speak.

At the hotel, Abraham requested a moment alone with Isaac. Father and son went to the Cohens' room. Sarah remained with Elder Gunther in the hotel lobby.


Abraham closed the door and pressed its lock. He sat on the bed and then stood and paced.

"You were rude to my friends," Isaac murmured. "You shamed me before my friends. *Lashon haraar*."

Abraham turned to him, eyes ablaze. "You shamed me before my God! Do not speak Hebrew to me; your mouth is not worthy to utter its holy words! I brought you the Law. From the fires of Sinai and Auschwitz, I brought you the Law, and I found you worshipping the gods of our enslavers! I brought you the Law, and you spurned it. Then have it not!"

"God gave the Law, not you."

"Yes, God! The God who chose Israel!"

"I don't expect you to understand—"

"I gave you our prayers, our heritage, our God. And you—"

"I love our prayers and our heritage and our God. Papa—"

"And you—you teach these goyim about your Jesus Christ—you tell them that the Jews—my people—called a curse upon their heads by supporting the execution of a man who had defiled the law and denigrated our priests. You, who should have been the joy of my old age, you have shamed me, Isaac, before my God! Tell me, were these Arabs, these PLO murderers, fulfilling the curse of Calvary as well?"

"Papa—"

"Did God tell them to kill those boys because the ancient Jews dared support the crucifixion of a heretic? Was God in charge of the murder of our boys?"

"No," Isaac moaned. "How can you ask it?"

"Did you see their bodies? Young, strong bodies. The best of our boys!"

"I saw."

"Did you?"

"Yes!"

"On the television, perhaps, you saw—or you think you saw their bodies. All neatly shrouded and shrunk to fit television technology. But you did not see their bodies. You did not see them as I did."

"I saw them."

"Did you?" Abraham demanded. "Think! Did you? Did you see their bones? Their arms reaching out like winter trees? Their tortured bones? Did you see? Did you feel their weight? And do you know who carried them from their death chambers? Do you? Your father carried them! I carried them! I carried them from the death traps! I looked into their dead eyes, breathed the odor of their extermination. It was I!"

"Papa—"

"They were my sons! My sons! My dead sons!"

"Please, Papa."

"Oh God, Master of the Universe, God—I carried them, burned them—I—"

"That was thirty years ago," Isaac said weakly.

"That was yesterday!" He roared the words.

"Yesterday. Papa—"

"Oh, I ache," Abraham murmured, hunching over, clutching his stomach. "Master of the Universe, I ache! My shoulders ache from bearing so much death. Death weighs down on me, Master of the Universe, death weighs me down!" He collapsed onto the bed.

"Papa, you're not making sense."

"And how do you want that I should make sense?" Abraham shouted, not looking up. "By letting your impotent little god snatch my tefillin? Or strangle me with my tallith until I convert? Is that how you want that I should make sense?" Now he raised his eyes to Isaac and then raised himself from the bed and began to pace vigorously.

"Don't speak like this, Papa. Don't—don't! I'm still your son."

"And Absalom was David's. Did you see their bodies? Did you?" He stopped before his son, challenged him with demanding eyes.

"Yes, I saw."

"Did you see with your whole soul? Smell with your whole soul? Did their death rattles echo through your whole soul? Did you feel the weight of their dead bodies?"

"Yes!" he shouted, louder than his father. "Yes, I did! I felt them here!" He brought his fist hard to his forehead. "And here!" He grabbed his forearm. "And here!" He pounded his fist to his heart.

Abraham stared hard at him, then spoke softly. "I know your friend, this Sell. But when I knew him, he could walk. Walk, yes. March. Trample. Crack a whip. He was there, at Auschwitz, on the other side. He was there, may God curse him!"

"No, Papa," breathed Isaac. "No. He was never in a camp. He was at the front. He was hurt at the Russian front."

"He was at Auschwitz," hissed Abraham. "They were all there. All the Germans who wore the swastika were there in the camp. All of them!"

"Herr Sell is my friend. He is *mein Brüder*."

"Then sleep with Hitler!" Abraham cried, the words ringing off the wall, making the lamp tremble. "Sleep with Hitler!"

Isaac stepped back, as though blown back by his father's fury. The room seemed to shiver and then grew deathly still. Isaac murmured something unintelligible.

"What?" said Abraham.

"Papa, please. Don't do this." Isaac's eyes filled as he approached his father, his arms rising. Abraham did not respond, and Isaac let his arms drop. "They have suffered too, the Sells have. Frau Sell's sister lives on the other side of the wall, in

East Berlin. She can't see her or be with her. She watched the wall go up brick by brick until her sister's face disappeared behind it. She lives with this pain every day."

"Why are you saying this to me? You want me to pity that woman who watched as MY loved ones were put on trains, babies torn from their mothers' breasts, and sent to die? You want me to weep that this German woman can't touch her sister's hand? My sister was raped and murdered while this German woman — and all her kind, all of them! — watched. And my firstborn child was —. No, I will not speak such things to you. You could never understand them. You want me to cry for Mrs. Sell? Her life is so pathetic to you, yes? This is why you tell me about the wall?"

"No, Papa. I tell you because I feel it in this room, here, between us — so high I can barely see your face and you can barely hear my voice. Or if my words are clear, they are flat, coming through rock. I hate this wall, Papa. I want it gone."

"Who built the wall? Eh? Who?"

"Who built it? It doesn't matter; it's there! And you will not help me tear it down unless I do the one thing I cannot do. To leave my faith would be to betray everything *you* have taught me about being true to what I know in myself is right. To leave my faith would be to remove my heart."

"And so you remove mine instead."

"You will never understand the decision I made, Papa — or its pain. The only answer I have to all you are saying, to all you are suffering, is that I love you. I love you," he repeated, mouth quivering, tears spilling. "And I love — I LOVE — those murdered men from Israel. Them, too! Please try to hear me. Please try to hear all that's behind my words. I did feel their deaths. I did! I felt them as I would have the death of a brother.

I am your son, Papa." He wept. "Please! Help me! Don't let the wall grow! Don't let it!" He raised his arms once more.

Abraham watched him for a long moment and then looked away.

"Papa, don't cast me off," Isaac said. "God meant me to be your son."

Abraham turned back to him. "Why should God give me such a son?" he asked emotionally.

"Don't cast me off, Papa. You must believe that God will provide himself a lamb for the offering. You must believe that, and put away the knife of your anger. Papa?"

"Isaac of old did all his father asked."

"Isaac of old loved God better than life. As did his father! And when the angel said, 'Lay not thy hand upon the lad,' Abraham obeyed. He knew there was purpose in all that had happened. Do you believe less than this, my father, my rabbi? Do you believe God has no plan for us? God gave me to you for a reason. Will you sacrifice me before you know what it is? Papa, I tell you, you are killing me this moment."

Abraham's eyes were fixed on Isaac's ready arms.

"Papa?"

Abraham closed his eyes. He looked like he was praying. When he opened them, they had softened and grown moist. Slowly, hesitantly, he raised his arms to the level of his son's. "Come," he said. "Come, then." Isaac fell into his father's embrace, and Abraham took him in, held him, rocked him as in a slow prayer. "I swore I would never again worship the idol of hatred," Abraham breathed. "The Lord is my God; the Lord is one. I shall have no other gods before Him. Never again. Never again." And then in German he repeated the words, the first in the language of his childhood he had spoken since the end of the war. "*Nie wieder.*"

Isaac was sobbing now. "They were my brothers."

"Of course they were. They were my sons," Abraham said.

"I carried them too."

"We all did. We all ache from their weight."

"I love you, Papa. I have broken your heart, I know. That pain is part of me forever. Part of us, who we are."

Abraham pressed his cheek to his son's. "Isaac, you are not what I wanted you to be. I do not, will not ever understand you. But you are still a gift from God to me, complete with pain, as God's gifts usually are. The first true prayer I spoke after my deliverance from Auschwitz was when I held your little body in my arms. You were so light and so alive. Your life filled my emptiness. God gave you to me to restore my soul. And I must keep my soul alive though I lose you completely. That is the Almighty's message to Abraham. His 'purpose,' as you said." He kissed Isaac's cheek and then looked upwards. "Master of the Universe," he said. "Behold! Here am I!"

When Isaac and Abraham entered the lobby, Sarah could tell they had been crying. She recalled Abraham's words: "I will never stop hoping that my son will be returned to me," and remembered Joseph of Egypt. Joseph was not returned to his father, but his father was conveyed to him in Egypt — yes, in Egypt. And she and Abraham had come to Isaac in Hamburg.

# CHAPTER 31

Isaac's mission ended in September 1972. He had baptized only one person in his two years in Germany — the sixteen-year-old girl who had had a crush on him.

On the final day of his mission, he sat in the airport beside Elder Gunther, who would be going home with him. Elder Gunther, whom he loved.

From the standpoint of statistics, his service had not yielded much fruit. But he had served with his whole soul. He had learned to love the people — even the Sells — and to love his God. Within him, something that had always been unbalanced was balanced now. The wellsprings of his feelings had been purified. The restoration was true.

Elsa did not meet Isaac at the airport, and he did not call

her until he had been home for two days. Even then, he stared long and hard at the phone before dialing. Elsa answered after the second ring, just as he was ready to hang up. He heard her familiar voice. "Hello?"

He opened his mouth.

"Hello?" she repeated.

"Hi."

"Isaac," she sighed, "what took you so long to call?"

"I don't know."

"Are you released?"

"Yes. Even honorably, believe it or not."

"I want to see you."

"I want to see you, too."

"In the library?"

"Good. In the library."

"Auf Wiedersehen," she said.

"Auf Wiedersehen."


It was a haunting, unnerving deja vu. Again, it seemed, Isaac was a high school student, headed for a rendezvous with the lovely shiksa. And Elsa—Elsa.

There she was, looking just the same as the last time he had seen her. Long, gleaming, platinum hair. Bright blue eyes. Cheeks shining.

"Dr. Livingston, I presume," she said, smiling nervously.

"Hello, Elsa."

"Hello, Isaac."

He sat on the chair beside her. Neither spoke for a long moment. She moved her hand to his head and stroked his hair. He sighed and embraced her.

"Do you think the librarians remember us?" asked Elsa, wiping her eyes.

"How could they forget?"

She took his hand and squeezed it. She stroked his fingers. "I'm so proud of you, Isaac," she said.

"I'm—thank you."

"I wasn't a very loyal lady-in-waiting."

"Doesn't matter. I was probably a better missionary after I got the 'Dear John.' "

"I never stopped loving you."

"I never stopped loving you, either."

She kissed his cheek and suggested they go out for hamburgers.

Over the next three months, Elsa and Isaac dated several times a week. They got engaged over Christmas, and chose June 1 as the day they would be married in the Salt Lake Temple.

Abraham was sitting in the armchair in his study when Isaac approached him.

"I have news," Isaac said.

"Is this news I should be sitting to receive?"

"I think it won't come as much of a surprise."

"Go on."

"Elsa and I have decided to get married."

Abraham nodded. "You're right. That's not much of a surprise. You spend so much time with a girl, it is natural that feelings develop and you want to get married."

"She is a good girl."

"She is not the one I would have chosen for you, you know that. If I were allowed to make your decisions for you, you would marry a fine, Jewish girl under the canopy. But, if this is your decision, I know you will keep to it. So, you and Elsa have decided to get married."

"Yes."

"When?"

"June first."

"Where?"

"The Salt Lake Temple."

"The Mormon temple in Salt Lake?"

"Yes."

"That should be very interesting. I have never been inside a Mormon temple."

Isaac breathed in sharply. "You can't go inside it," he blurted. "Only Mormons in good standing can go inside it."

"What?"

"Only Mormons," he murmured.

"You are saying I cannot attend your wedding? You are telling me I cannot attend my own son's wedding?"

"Outside the temple, Elsa and I will exchange rings. We want you present for that."

"But the wedding itself I cannot attend?"

"The wedding itself, you cannot attend." He looked down.

"You would reject our ways and your own parents so thoroughly?"

"Papa—"

"Do you know—can you imagine—how a father looks forward to his son's wedding? Of all the celebrations, marriage is the most joyous, the most awaited. Please—please, Isaac . . . please tell your mother I wish to speak with her. Leave me."

Isaac slipped out the door. Sarah entered.

"So, you know about his plans?" said Abraham, his hands flat on his desk.

"Yes."

"And what do you think?"

"That it doesn't matter what I think. Isaac is a man. We must treat him as a man. He will do what he wants to anyway."

"Support I will not give. Only tolerance."

"That is all that is required of you."

"It seems to be all and everything. The theme of my life."

"Yes."

"I will never believe that the Almighty wanted my son — our son — to abandon the faith we have given him, to become — God forbid — a convert. But the Master of all will never undo his children's freedom no matter the grief it brings him. And God teaches us lessons from the circumstances. God has chosen, it seems, to teach me tolerance. No, of course I will not stand in the way of my son. God forbid I should force my son to do righteousness. Tell Isaac to come in again."

Sarah left, returning a minute later with Isaac at her side.

Abraham forced a smile. "So, you want to marry Elsa."

"Yes," Isaac answered.

"In the Mormon temple in Salt Lake City, Utah, where only Mormons can enter?"

"Yes."

Abraham puckered his mouth and nodded. "It is your wedding, not mine."

"I'm happy for you, Isaac," said Sarah.

"At least," said Abraham, "make us lots of grandchildren."

# CHAPTER 32

The wedding day was bright and full of lilacs. The Cohens and the Grubbes had all flown to Salt Lake City the night before.

The marriage ceremony was to be held at eleven in the morning. The wedding party arrived at Temple Square two hours early. Isaac wanted them all there early so he could show his parents the temple, the Visitors Center, the Tabernacle.

As it happened, the Tabernacle Choir was practicing. Abraham stopped when he heard the music, and leaned against a large willow tree as he listened.

> The Lord is my Shepherd; no want shall I know.
> I feed in green pastures, safe folded I rest.
> He leadeth my soul where the still waters flow,
> Restores me when wandering, redeems when oppressed;
> Restores me when wandering, redeems when oppressed.

Through the valley and shadow of death though I stray,
Since thou art my Guardian, no evil I fear.
Thy rod shall defend me, thy staff be my stay . . .

Abraham stood reverently, supported by the tree, as the notes faded. "This is good, this music," he said. "That choir is world famous, you know. Sarah, did you hear the music?"

"Yes," she said softly, looking not at Abraham but at the grown weeping willow he leaned against. She remembered another willow tree: a young, immature, crystallized tree that had spoken to her when she was a child. "Yes," she repeated, "I heard. I heard." She moved her eyes from the willow to the temple. Abraham's gaze followed hers.

"The temple," said Isaac. "It took forty years to build."

"Oh? The same number of years the Israelites wandered in the wilderness before being allowed to take the promised land," said Abraham, adding, "Someone in the Heavens must like that number."

"The pioneers who built this temple wandered in the wilderness, too, Papa," said Isaac. "They had settled in Ohio, a place called Kirtland, and they had built a temple there. But sin invaded the temple, and the Spirit of God could not stay in it. Apostates took it over. It was turned into a barn."

"A barn!" Abraham echoed.

"The pioneers settled in Illinois next," Isaac continued. "A place called Nauvoo."

"Nauvoo?"

"Yes. 'The City Beautiful.' "

"A Hebrew name."

"Yes. A Hebrew name."

"And they built another temple there?"

"An even costlier one than the first, requiring even more

time, even more sacrifice. And soon after it was completed, it was destroyed."

"Your temple was destroyed too?"

"Mobs pillaged the city and burned the temple."

"Mobs seem to enjoy burning temples. And the Mormon people—they let it burn?"

"Yes, Papa. I think maybe God requires us sometimes to let a temple burn as sacrifice. Sometimes, I think, we must allow the temple to burn and then let God teach us how to restore it. And this," said Isaac, motioning to the temple, "this for us is the restoration. But it did not come easily. The pioneers wandered in the wilderness, spent lives on the plains, and came here, to this desert. Then, through their faith, they moved this mountain. It is granite, mixed with all the work and tears the Lord required. Forty years of work."

"And so," said Abraham, "this is where you will be married."

"Yes."

Again, music wafted from the Tabernacle: a solo from Handel's *Messiah*: "O thou that tellest good tidings to Zion . . . get thee up into the high mountain . . . arise; shine; for thy light is come."

Sarah could not keep from looking at Elsa. The word *shine* seemed answered in her. Yes, shine, radiant, radiant bride.

The choir joined the soloist: "O thou that tellest good tidings to Zion—arise, arise! The glory of the Lord is risen upon thee."

Sarah looked up to the temple spires, where the gleaming gold angel was poised, silently trumpeting his glad tidings upon the high mountain.

"It's time, Isaac," said Elsa, as the music changed again to a quiet "Amen" chorus.

Sarah opened her arms to the bride. Abraham followed suit, and then turned to his son, shook his hand, and embraced him. "Now go," Sarah said, kissing Isaac's cheek, "go and get married."

"We'll meet here at 11:30," said Isaac. "We'll exchange rings then."

Abraham waved him on. "Yes, yes. You go now."

The bride and groom, followed by the Grubbe family, entered the temple.

"So," said Abraham. "So this is Temple Square in Salt Lake City, Utah. It's a nice place, isn't it, Sarah?"

"Very nice," she said.

They looked once more at the temple and then went into the Visitors Center.

A guide, whom Sarah acknowledged as "a nice-looking boy," showed them murals from the Old Testament and the New Testament. He then illuminated a simulated grove, where a wigged mannequin knelt. He explained that it represented Joseph Smith, a modern-day prophet.

The guide led them next to the huge, white *Christus,* and declared that this was a representation of Jesus Christ, the Messiah.

At this, the rabbi smiled. "The man Jesus was a Jew. This statue looks like a Scandinavian."

"The original was done by a Dane," the guide admitted.

"But Jesus was a Jew," said Abraham gently. "He was a Jew."

The guide nodded. "Yes, I know. He was a Jew."

At 11:45, Isaac and Elsa, both dressed in white, came from the temple. Sarah and Abraham embraced them again.

"We'll exchange rings now," said Isaac.

Abraham held out his hand. "Wait," he said. "I know you are Mormons, and I am and will always be of the Jewish faith. And I know a rabbi has no authority in a Mormon setting. Still, I am your father. I do have authority by virtue of that. Isaac, Elsa, let me call upon the Master of the Universe through the avenues of my faith to bless you."

"Please," said the newlyweds.

Slowly, the rabbi's body swayed. He recited a psalm and then said, "My son, if this were a Jewish wedding, you would crush a glass in remembrance of the destruction of our temple. For you—" he looked at the sparkling mountain "—for you, perhaps you don't remember the destruction of your temple, since this one is—since it has been restored to you. I think maybe there is good in this. Maybe it is good to remember that in his own time and in his own way, God restores whatever man destroys. Therein is your hope. And mine."

The bride and groom took hands.

"Put the ring on her finger, Isaac." It was a simple ring, a thin circle of gold. "And you, my daughter, give him his ring." Elsa slipped the ring onto Isaac's finger. "Now, my son, your ways are different from my ways. But God's words are for all of us. I tell you now, in all your ways, acknowledge Him, and let him teach you HIS ways. The Lord bless you and keep you. The Lord make his face to shine upon you, and be gracious unto you." Abraham smiled. "*Mazel tov*," he said.

"*Mazel tov*," echoed Sarah.

Music from the Tabernacle filled the air:

> Glory to God on high!
> Let heav'n and Earth reply
> Praise ye his name . . .

And somewhere, in the far reaches of her mind, it seemed to Sarah that she could hear a trumpet sounding.